**art** / shop / eat

# Paris

D0449806

Delia Gray-Durant

# ten things to do

[1] Zoom to the top of the Institut du Monde Arabe in a glass lift to enjoy the birdseye view of Notre-Dame de Paris and the Ile-de-la-Cité (*see p. 86*).

[2] Splurge on a gourmet meal in Le Grand Véfour, the oldest and most charming restaurant in Paris. Be sure to reserve a table in the main room (*see p. 51*).

[3] Stop and think for a moment inside the sculpture garden at Musée Rodin, the most popular museum in Paris devoted to a single artist, where Auguste Rodin worked and lived (*see p. 121*).

[4] Sip a *café crème* in the famous writers' haunts of the city such as Brasserie Lipp (*see p. 99*), Les Deux Magots and Café de Flore (*see p. 103*). Or stock up on some literary inspiration from the bookshop, Shakespeare and Co. (*see p. 106*).

**[5]** Plunge into Monet's *Waterlilies* at the Orangerie, for an all-enveloping art experience (*see p. 47*).

**[6]** Indulge in some top class retail therapy at the grandiose Printemps department store. If you have real shopping stamina, there is the equally magnificent Galeries Lafayette close by (*see p. 59*).

**[7]** Get on your skates and roller-blade with thousands of Parisians: or at least go to cheer them on. Steady skaters meet at 10pm on Fridays, in Place Raoul Dautry, Montparnasse; the wobblies at 2pm on Sundays, on Boulevard Bourdon, Bastille, www.parisinfo.com

**[8]** Climb to the top of the hillock in the Jardin des Plantes to find the oldest metal structure in Paris, the Gloriette (1786), designed by Edmé Verniquet (*see p. 94*).

**[9]** Relax on the beach in the city centre when 'Paris Plage' appears on 3km of the Right Bank of the Seine near the Hôtel de Ville in July and August.

**[10]** Walk on both levels of the Passerelle Léopold Sédar Senghor, the beautiful single-span footbridge which links the Jardin des Tuileries (*see p. 50*) and the Musée d'Orsay (*see p. 112*).

# contents

## About this guide

This book is for those who want to learn more about Paris's richly endowed museums and exceptional monuments, but for whom the other good things in life such as great shops, excellent food and a comfortable place to stay, are just as important.

The contents are divided into four main sections each of which could be the basis of a pleasant day's walk or provide the background for several days' more detailed exploration: a selection of the major **art** sights is given, then some other things to see **in the area**, followed by a few ideas on the **eat** opportunities, rounded off with our shortlist of **shop** recommendations.

In the **practicalities** section we give a brief introduction to the city of Paris, how to get around, its food and drink and where to stay. The **history** pages give an overview of the key events in this city's life, while at the back of the book there is a **glossary** covering some of the art terms and key personalities referred to in the guide, as well as a comprehensive **index** to help you find what you are looking for.

There are excellent **maps** throughout, on the inside cover is a map of all Paris clearly indicating where the detailed maps to each district are to be found at the beginning of their sections. The numbers (**①**) on the maps locate the cafés and restaurants described later in that section.

Enjoy Paris and do not hesitate to contact us with any views, recommendations or corrections: **www.blueguides.com**

# practicalities

## INTRODUCTION

Whose heart doesn't miss a beat at the sight of the steely Parisian icon, the Eiffel Tower, whether for the first or the fifteenth time, or is not moved at the magnificence of the Louvre Palace and the audacious crystal Pyramid at its core. Such monuments create the backdrop to a city whose many-facetted charm is in a constant state of renewal and flux. Discovery or rediscovery, there is something for everyone in Paris.

New on the culture scene are the Musée Branly, focusing on primitive arts and ethnology, in Jean Nouvel's innovative building, and the Cité de l'Architecture et du Patrimoine in the Palais de Chaillot in 2007. Much-loved museums, dark for some years, such as the Musée des Arts Décoratifs, the Musée de l'Orangerie, the Musée du Petit Palais and the city's modern art collections in the Palais de Tokyo, have been revealed in all their glory. The gourmet visitor will find endless reinventions by top chefs such as Hélène Darroze and Joël Robuchon (*see p. 124*) in the cuisine and restaurants, as well as in stores such as Pierre Hermé's ultra-trendy pâtisserie (*see p. 106*), Michel Cluizel's La Fontaine au Chocolat (*see p. 56*), or Fromagerie 31 (*see p. 104*) which is not just a simple cheese shop. The hottest fashion trends veer towards the concept store, of which Colette (*see p. 57*) is considered the most 'progressive' although the specialty boutique is still reliably present in all forms. As for outdoor activities, Parisians have taken to their roller blades and to sunbathing on the sandy Paris Plage, and in summer there are numerous street fairs and open-air entertainment.

## GETTING THERE

**Eurostar** trains leave from London Waterloo (until 14 November 2007, when the service moves to London St Pancras), and from Ashford International, Kent. Trains arrive at Gare du Nord in Paris, approximately 2hr 40mins later.

**Roissy-Charles de Gaulle Airport** (CDG), Tel: 0891 68 15 15, www.adp.fr. Air France Coaches run every 15mins to Etoile (*map p. 24, B1*) from 5.45am–11pm; and every 30mins from CDG to Gare de Lyon (*map p. 63, D4*) and Gare Montparnasse from 7am–9pm. Roissybus runs every 15–20mins from CDG to Opéra-Rue Scribe (*map p. 25, A2*), from 6am–11pm; and in the opposite direction every 15–20mins from 5.45am–11pa. A suburban train (RER Line B) runs every 8mins, from CDG to Gare du Nord, from 5.44am–midnight, and in the opposite direction from 4.56am–midnight.

**Orly Airport**, Tel: 0892 68 15 15, www.adp.fr. Air France Coaches run every 15mins from Orly to Gare Montparnasse, from 6am–11pm and in the opposite direction from 5.45am–11pm. Orlyval shuttle train runs every 7mins, connecting with RER B at Antony, from 6am–11pm. RER Line C (plus ADP shuttle bus) runs every 15mins from Orly–Paris, 5.50am–10.50pm and in the opposite direction from 5.45am–11.15pm.

## GETTING AROUND

The Paris Convention and **Visitors Bureaux** main office is at 25 Rue des Pyramides, Metro: Pyramides, Tuileries, Tel: 0892 68 3000, www.parisinfo.com. There are also branches at: 11 Rue Scribe, Metro: Opéra; 20 Boulevard Diderot, Metro: Gare-de-Lyon; Avenue des Champs-Elysées/Avenue Marigny, Metro: Champs-Elysées-Clémenceau. There is also a tourist office at Carrousel du Louvre, 99 Rue de Rivoli, Metro: Palais-Royal, Musée-du-Louvre, www.pidf.com.

Parisian public transport is run by RATP (www.ratp.fr). The **Métro** runs frequently between 5.30am and 12.30am. The 14 lines are identifiable by their number and colour. The **RER** (suburban express railway) is a fast under- and overground service with 5 lines: A, B, C, D and E. **Bus** routes are numbered and most operate 6.30am–8.30pm (a few until 12.30am). Routes and timetables are shown at individual bus stops. Night buses run from 1am–5.35am.

The same **tickets** are used on the Métro, RER within central Paris, and buses. They can be purchased individually or in tens (*carnet*) at all RATP stations and some tobacconists. Travel passes offering unlimited travel by public transport are also available. Paris-Visite travel pass is valid for 1, 2, 3 or 5 consecutive days of unlimited travel by Métro, RER, bus, suburban SNCF trains and Montmartre Funicular and includes reductions to numerous sites and L'Open Tour. Mobilis is an unlimited stop-go one-day pass for Métro, RER and bus covering zones 1–2 up to 1–8 (excluding airports).

**Taxis** have no distinctive form or colour and have a white 'Taxi' sign on the roof (lit when available). A supplement is charged for luggage placed in the boot; no supplement for wheelchairs.

There are various **tour coaches** in the city. A special line, Balabus runs April–Sept, 12.30–8pm, and covers tourist sites between Bastille and La Défense; stops are marked Balabus (Bb). Paris l'Open Tour, www.paris-opentour.com is a sightseeing/hop-on-hop-off service.

**River cruises** can be taken with Batobus, Port de la Bourdonnais, Metro: Bir-Hakeim, Tel: 01 44 11 33 99, www.batobus.com, which offers 8 stops on the Seine. Other companies include: Bateaux Parisiens, Tel: 01 44 11 33 44, www.bateauxparisiens.com; Capitaine Fracasse/Le Grand Bleu, Tel: 01 46 21 48 15, www.quai55.com; La Marina de Paris, Tel: 01 43 43 40 30, www.marinadeparis.com; Vedettes de Pont-Neuf, Tel: 01 46 33 98 38, www.pontneuf.net.

## ENTERTAINMENT

For up-to-date online listings, see www.parisinfo.com. The weekly publications *Pariscope* and *l'Officiel des Spectacles* also have entertainment sections. For the opera, go to www.opera-de-paris.fr or www.opera-comique.com. For other types of music go to www.cite-musique.fr or www.sallepleyel.fr. Tickets for major events can be purchased at FNAC outlets in Paris, www.fnac.fr; Virgin-Megastores at Carrousel du Louvre and Champs-Elysées. Half-price ticket kiosks can be found at 15 Place de la Madeleine (*Map p. 25, B1*) and web sites as above.

## SHOPS

Shops are usually open from 9 or 10am until 6 or 7pm. Fashion stores are generally closed on Sunday and some on Monday morning.

Food shops often open earlier and stay open until 7, and some open Sunday morning.

There are **markets** all over Paris (see www.paris.fr). There is a famous flower market on Place Louis-Lépine on the Ile de la Cité (*map p. 84, A3*) which on Sundays becomes a bird market while opposite, on Quai de la Mégisserie, are pet shops. Buying food for a picnic is no problem: *charcutiers* (cooked meats), *traiteurs* (caterers) and *épiceries* (grocers) are the traditional up-market 'take-aways', and many *boulangeries* (bakers) make sandwiches, quiches and tarts to go.

## FOOD & DRINK

Paris has prided itself on its food for centuries, and while you won't hear many Parisians echoing the Italian claim that use of knives and forks only arrived with the civilizing influence of Catherine de Medici—she came from Florence to marry the French king Henri II in the 16th century—it is certain that a major contributor to Paris's superb restaurant scene was the Revolution at the end of the 18th century. Neither the aristocrats who fled from it nor those that stayed to be guillotined could offer much in the way of employment to their armies of cooks, many of whom turned to providing their exquisite meals in public premises with individual tables, a choice of

**A typical bistro in Paris**

dishes and good service to earn a living. As part of the same move-ment it became a matter of pride for citizens to demonstrate how un-aristocratic they were by being seen to eat in the growing number of public taverns.

Restaurant, café, bistro and brasserie are all familiar labels for places to eat, and it may not be a surprise that most have a French origin. From the 16th century, the word **restaurant** was used to describe a restorative soup but the word as we now understand it appeared in the 18th century. A soupseller called Boulanger was the first in Paris to promote 'restaurants', in the 1860s, which referred to different dishes served in his tavern, including *ragout* of sheep's feet. The forerunner of today's style of restaurant was La Grande Taverne de Londres, opened in Paris in 1782 by Antoine Beauvilliers whose spreading reputation for fine food made him one of the world's first celebrity chefs. The Age of Enlightenment's concerns with health, diet and cooking, contributed to the spread of restaurants. The oldest and one of the most beautiful restaurants in Paris today opened in 1784 as the Café de Chartres and is now the well-known Le Grand Véfour (*see p. 51*).

All types of **café** abound, and are inextricably associated with cof-fee drinking. The word comes from the French, which itself is from the Arabic for strength or vigour, *qhawa* transformed into *kaweh* in the Ottoman Empire and *caffé* by French explorers. The oldest café in Paris is Le Procope (*see p. 100*), from the start a place to drink coffee, read papers and converse—especially about politics.

The word '**bistro**' was not recorded until the late 1800s. Its origin may have been from a northern French colloquial term *bistouill'* or *bistrouille*, a mixture of coffee and brandy or, bad alcohol; alterna-tively, it may come from a regional expression, *bistraud*, meaning an under-servant. Who knows? The bistro is usually seen as an unpre-tentious, inexpensive place to eat traditional dishes such as *steak au poivre*, French onion soup and *coq au vin*, and still is on the Ile de la Cité at Le Vieux Bistrot (*see p. 103*). And **brasseries** do still exist, the word coming from *brasser*, to malt, but while they no longer brew they do normally serve beer on tap. These frequently large and hand-some establishments were established around the turn of the 19th and 20th centuries, and were kitted out with splendid Belle Epoque, Art

Nouveau or Art Deco decoration, mirrors, bright lights, and rows of tables. Because of their popularity and rapid service at any time of day, they tended (and still do) to be noisy and hectic and serve traditional food.

Many Paris restaurants boast some regional (French) specialisation, others offer 'typical' Parisian food, which is traditionally rather elaborate although the *nouvelle cuisine* which started thirty years ago marked a move back to cleaner tastes. The **menu** in French means a fixed-price (and usually cheaper) short selection of two or three daily choices, **carte** refers to what would be called a menu in English, **à la carte** offers an extended choice rather than sticking with the dishes of the day. The *menu* will traditionally start with an **entrée**, or starter, such as *charcuterie*, cold meat cuts, *crudités*, raw vegetables, or *pâté*. They will be followed by a **plat principal**, a main dish of meat or fish with vegetables, then **fromage**, cheese: *brie* is from the area of the old royal palace southwest of Paris at Fountainebleau, *brie de Melun* tends to be stronger in taste and smell and more salted than the larger and creamier *brie de Meaux*. The meal ends with **dessert** which in the Paris region is often pastry based.

As for drink, a meal is preceded by an **apéritif** which is traditionally a vermouth, dry or sweet fortified wine flavoured with herbs and spices, accompanied by *vin*, wine, and ended with a **digestif**, generally brandy or one of the branded 'stickies' such as the orange based Grand Marnier or Cointreau, to aid the digestion.

Some of the most famous **wines** are French and familiar from the wine lists of the world's capitals: Bordeaux, or historically 'claret' for the British; Burgundy and Chateau Neuf du Pape, mainly reds from the southwest, central east and south of the country respectively; Champagne; Chablis, a steely, chardonnay-based white wine from the north of France; and the sweet dessert wine Sauternes. Some lesser known regions are becoming increasingly popular, such as the Rhone, or the Loire with its subtle, lighter reds such as Chinon. A few years ago it was felt that these historic French wines were becoming tired and overtaken by fruitier, more muscular New World wines—from Australia, New Zealand, California, Argentina—but this competition has benefited not only the top wines in France, which have had to prove themselves, but also the *vins de pays,* 'country', wines, particularly

**Relaxing Parisian style, in the pavement cafés of the city**

those from the sunny Mediterranean south—Languedoc and Rousillon—as well as the southwest, inland from Bordeaux, for example Gaillac and Cahors. These wines match the New World wines in quality and value for money.

Recommended **restaurants** are given in each section of this book. Our favourite restaurants carry the Blue Guides Recommended sign: ■ (see www.blueguides.com for details). Categories are according to price per person for dinner, with wine:

| | |
|---|---|
| €€€€ | €100+ |
| €€€ | €50–€100 |
| €€ | €30–€50 |
| € | under €30 |

## WHERE TO STAY

Paris has over 2,000 hotels with some 75,000 rooms in a huge range of styles, value and prices. There is a tourist tax which may or may not be included in the quoted price. Breakfasts are rarely included, unless on special offers.

In this section you will find a small selection of the accommodation available in Paris. Hotels that are particularly good (in terms of location, charm and value for money) carry the Blue Guides Recommended sign: ■ (see www.blueguides.com for details). The prices below are a guideline only for a double room in high season:

| | |
|---|---|
| €€€ | €300+ |
| €€ | €200–300 |
| € | below €200 |

**€€€ Hotel Costes**. *239 Rue St-Honore, Tel: 01 42 44 50 00, www.hotelcostes.com, 82 rooms, Metro: Tuileries. Map p. 25, C2.* An utterly exclusive hotel which draws the celebrities. The discreet entrance is dark, moody and mysterious—entering the hotel takes you into a world of glamour and opulence. Yet it retains an air of intimacy, with small spaces around a very beautiful interior courtyard. And to help you keep in shape, you can swim to music in the gorgeous oriental style pool and exercise in the fitness centre. The restaurant is worth trying (*see p. 51*).

**€€€ L'Hôtel**. ■ *Rue des Beaux-Arts, Tel: 01 44 41 99 00, www.l-hotel.com, 30 rooms,* *Metro: St-Germaine-des-Prés. Map p. 84, A1.* This is an attractive boutique hotel in a building which carries lots of historic baggage yet is up-to-the-minute. Architecturally, its unique characteristic is a 6-storey circular balconied atrium above ancient stone cellars. Owned by Peter Frankopan and Jessica Sainsbury (Cowley Manor in the UK is another of their properties), this has been a hotel of distinction since the time of Oscar Wilde who famously drew his last breath here in 1900. Fashionable designer Jacques Garcia has carried out the latest transformation, bringing a different theme to each of the bedrooms: from the legendary Wilde bedroom, with English furniture and a peacock mural, to the Cardinal room with a view of the belfry of St-Germain, and the Restoration-style Roi de Naples room. The lounge, bar and restaurant are intimate and comfortable and lead to a courtyard with a fountain.

€€€ **Hôtel Lutetia**. *46 Boulevard Raspail, Tel: 01 49 54 46 46, www.lutetia-paris.com, 250 rooms, Metro: Rue du Bac. Map p. 109, B8.* A grand and traditional hotel built in 1910 at the instigation of the owner of the Bon Marché department store, which is opposite. The Lutetia has belonged to the Tattinger family since 1955, but now comes under the Concorde hotel umbrella. It has seen its fair share of celebrities—Picasso, Matisse, Josephine Baker and General de Gaulle among them. The first Art Deco hotel in Paris, it has kept its authentic style inside and out. All of the huge bedrooms and suites are beautifully appointed and have 1930s-style furnishings, using tones of gold and mahogany. Some of the suites (Literary and Eiffel) have spectacular views towards the Eiffel Tower, and the Suite Opéra where the Director of Opéra Garnier lived for many years, is atmospheric in emerald green and light wood. There is a gastronomic restaurant 'Paris', a wonderfully authentic brasserie specialising in *fruits de mer*, and the glamorous Bar Lutece.

€€ **Hôtel Bourg Tibourg**. *19 Rue du Bourg Tibourg, Tel: 01 42 78 47 39, www.hotelbourg tibourg.com, 32 rooms, Metro: Hôtel de Ville. Map p. 63, B1.* In the heart of the Marais, boutiques, museums and Place des Vosges are almost on the doorstep. The designer Jacques Garcia is responsible for the neo-Viollet-le-Duc look in this luxurious hotel owned by the Frères Costes, and designed as a voyage in itself. No surface is ignored and no detail spared. The smallish, warmly coloured rooms have superb touches such as fringed lampshades and gilded fretwork. Black granite and mosaic tiles feature in the bathrooms. There is also a tiny garden with about room for two to breakfast. The whole effect is opulent and bordering on 19th-century up-market bordello.

€€ **Hôtel Buci**. *22 Rue de Buci, Tel: 01 55 42 74 74, www.hotel buci.fr, 24 rooms, Metro: St-Germaine-des-Prés. Map p. 84, B2.* This is a very charming hotel which has got the balance just right. Beautifully situated on a little street deep in St-Germain, close to the traditional Buci street market, as well as galleries, antiques shops and boutiques of the *quartier*, it occupies a 16th-century building. The very attractive entrance lobby sets the standard for the subtle and thoughtful décor with a comfortable, understated lounge. The breakfast room, which doubles up as a bar, is a small haven of tranquillity. No detail is spared in the decoration of the bedrooms, some with exposed beams, and marble bathrooms; the theme is luxurious but not overwhelming.

€€ **Hôtel Edouard VII.** ▪ *39 Avenue de l'Opéra, Tel: 01 42 61 86 15, www.edouard7 hotel.com, 70 rooms, Metro: Opéra. Map p. 25, B2.* This is a very good hotel, one of two (with the Aviatic) owned by the Corbel family where quality, efficiency and excellent service are apparent throughout. Built in 1877, during the time of the Entente Cordiale, it was patronised by King Edward VII who enjoyed the view of the Opera House from the balconies. The lobby has an eclectic choice of décor

combining traditional marble, mahogany and Italian chandeliers with modern carvings by Nicolas Cesbron. Off the lobby is a very comfortable bar with the original stained-glass windows and modern furnishing. Meals, including the copious buffet breakfast, are served in the

**The stunning lobby of the Hôtel Edouard VII, built in the 19th century**

restaurant, Angl'Opéra (*see p. 52*). Suites have views of the Opera facade from their balconies. High-quality fabrics are a keynote of the Edouard VII. The bedrooms have been refurbished with wood parquet floors and deep luxurious colour schemes; bathrooms have granite floors, double basins, good lighting and bathrobes.

**€€ Hôtel du Jeu de Paume**. *54 Rue St-Louis-en-l'Ile, Tel: 01 43 26 14 18, www.hoteljeude-paume.com, 30 rooms, Metro: Ponte Marie. Map p. 84, B4.* A very classily converted 17th-century building where real tennis was once played. The tennis court is cleverly converted into the lounge with a painting of a game in progress. Modern features combine harmoniously with old beams and stone walls. The elegant bedrooms use subtle colours teamed with carefully selected antiques and old pieces. There are apartments for longer stays on the first and second floors at the front of the building, both equipped with kitchen and bathrooms.

**€ Hotel Aviatic.** ▪ *105 Rue de Vaugirard, Tel: 01 53 63 25 50, www.aviatic.fr, 32 rooms, Metro: St-Sulpice, Rennes. Map p. 84, C1.* This is a very comfortable period piece with the Tour Montparnasse nearby for a sky-high cocktail. It is owned by the Corbel family (who also own the Edouard VII; *see previous page*) and similar high standards prevail. A hotel since 1856, bedrooms are ingeniously and individually decorated with restored furniture and artefacts, and tasteful Pierre Frey fabrics. The entrance hall is typical of an old Parisian house, with a pretty staircase, and a small attractively decorated Empire-style lounge. The staff are helpful, and the breakfast room has a café atmosphere (good teabags).

**€ Hôtel de la Bretonnerie**. *Rue Ste-Croix-de-la-Bretonnerie, Tel: 01 48 87 77 63, www.breton-nerie.com, 28 rooms, Metro: Hôtel de Ville. Map p. 63, B1.* This is a delightful, intimate hotel deep in the Marais with a pretty entrance hall and a fine 17th-century staircase. Carefully chosen furniture projects a welcoming atmosphere. Although the old building does not allow for spacious rooms, each of the bedrooms or small suites is individually decorated in lush warm colours or chinzes in contrast with exposed beams and stone walls. The breakfast room is in the stone-vaulted undercroft.

The hotel is well situated for Place des Vosges and the museums of the Marais, which is one of the few places where many shops open on Sunday.

**€ Hôtel Brighton.** *Rue de Rivoli, Tel: 01 47 03 61 61, www.paris-hotel-brighton.com, 61 rooms, Metro: Tuileries. Map p. 25, C2.* The Brighton has been so called since the Entente Cordiale between England and France at the time of Queen Victoria. The interior retains much of its original 1850s charm, including faux-marble and mosaics. It has an excellent location, overlooking the Tuileries Gardens. The remarkably spacious rooms are good quality and quite traditional, with large bathrooms. Those at the back are quieter, but those on Rue de Rivoli have the advantage of the view. This hotel is excellent value considering the size of the rooms and the position.

**€ Hôtel Le Clément.** ■ *6 Rue Clément, Tel: 01 43 26 53 60, www.hotel-clement.fr, 28 rooms, Metro: Mabillon. Map p. 84, B1.* This is a gem of an independent hotel opposite the renovated Marché St-Germain shopping mall. Discreet, quiet, cosy, utterly charming (if you have a large suitcase it will probably have to travel alone in the lift) but perfectly presented. Bijou bedrooms have pretty prints on the walls and cane furniture. The brightest rooms overlook the street, room 106 is the smallest and 107 the quietest. From the 4th floor is a rooftop view including the belfry of St-Sulpice. In a brilliant situation within a stone's throw of St-Germain des Prés, there is great shopping all around.

**€ Hôtel des Grandes Ecoles.** *75 Rue du Cardinal Lemoine, Tel: 01 43 26 79 23, www.hotel-grandes-ecoles.com, 51 rooms, Metro: Cardinal Lemoine, Monge. Map p. 84, D3.* This budget hotel has a remarkable setting in the Latin Quarter, close to the Panthéon, the Jardin du Luxembourg and Rue Mouffetard. Its spacious rooms, somewhat chintzy and lacy, are in old buildings surrounding a garden; a little oasis of greenery. Breakfast is served in a light, sunny room in winter and outside in summer.

**€ Hôtel Lenox.** *9 Rue de l'Université, Tel: 01 42 96 10 95, www.lenoxsaintgermain.com, 34 rooms, Metro: Rue du Bac. Map p. 109, B8.* The theme of this old literary hotel is Art Deco leather upholstery and polished wood with a slightly masculine air, and the Lenox Club bar features marquetry images of jazz musicians. A glass elevator takes you to thoughtfully presented, uncluttered bedrooms. At the other extreme, the breakfast room is in the converted cellar. This is a great corner of St-Germain with its narrow streets, situated very close to the Musée d'Orsay and the river.

**€ Hôtel Louvre-Opéra**. *4 Rue des Moulins, Tel: 01 40 20 01 10, www.hotel-paris-louvre-opera.com, 20 rooms, Metro:* *Pyramide. Map p. 25, B3.* This new hotel occupies an old building, which has been totally renovated and refurbished, in a prestigious location on the Right Bank—as the name suggests. It is also close to the gardens of the Palais Royal and the Jardins des Tuileries, and to Place Vendôme. There is brilliant shopping and a vast range of restaurants in the vicinity, nevertheless this is a quiet street. Careful use of space has been made in the rooms, although bathrooms are a reasonable size.

**Comfortable interiors with restored furniture at the Hotel Aviatic**

**€ Hôtel de Nesle**. *7 Rue de Nesle, Tel: 01 43 54 62 41, www.hotel denesleparis.com, 20 rooms, Metro: Odéon. Map p. 84, A2.* This hotel is not for the faint-hearted, but if you are an insomniac you would think you were dreaming. A budget hotel tucked away in the Latin Quarter, with a mini garden. Between the Quai des Orfévres and Boulevard St-Germain, it is handy for the Ile de la Cité and St-Michel. The low prices reflect the minimal facilities and the rooms are decidedly quirky. Each has its own painted decor–Champollion is Egyptian and Antinéa has its own hammam. Some facilities are shared, and there is no breakfast but that's almost an advantage with all the local cafes, including La Procope, just around the corner.

**€ Hôtel de la Sorbonne**, *6 Rue Victor-Cousin, Tel: 01 43 54 58 08, www.hotelsorbonne.com, 39 rooms, Metro: Maubert Mutualité. Map p. 84, C2.* This is one of the better 2-star hotels in the capital, and the prices are very kind on the pocket. The ancient student quarter, close to the Pantheon, is a great area and the hotel is prettily turned out. The rooms have nice decorative touches teamed with simple furniture. The Panthéon can be glimpsed from some rooms.

**€ Hôtel de la Tulipe**. *33 Rue Malar, Tel: 01 45 51 67 21, www.hoteldelatulipe.com, 22 rooms, Metro: La Tour Maubourg. Map p. 108, A4.* This small, cheerful hotel with a Provençal feel, is in the shadow of the Eiffel Tower and close to lively shopping streets. Formerly a convent, the building is arranged around a small interior courtyard where breakfast tables are set out in the summer. Sunny, yellow fabrics contrast with old beams and stone walls. The rooms are simple, but well equipped and reasonably priced.

# history

## Beginnings

**3rd century BC** The Parisii, a Celtic tribe, inhabit islands on the Seine

**54 BC** The Romans overcome the Parisii and found the Gallo-Roman city of Lutetia

**c. 245 AD** St Denis establishes the Christian Church in Lutetia

**c. 258** St Denis martyred on the hill of Montmartre; legend claims he walked north to the site of his burial carrying his severed head

**357** Julian the Apostate becomes Prefect of the Gauls. The island becomes known as *Civitas Parisiorum*

**451** Ste Geneviève defends Paris against the Huns

**508** The Merovingians, under King Clovis, make Paris their capital

## The Middle Ages and the Renaissance

**1163** Notre-Dame Cathedral begun by Bishop Maurice de Sully on the Ile de la Cité (*see p. 86*)

**1180–1223** King Philippe-Auguste (Philippe II) builds a city wall and fortress on the Right Bank, later the Louvre Palace (*see p. 27*)

**1246–49** Louis IX (St-Louis) builds the royal chapel of Ste-Chapelle (*see p. 89*)

**1301–13** Philippe IV builds a palace on the Ile de la Cité, later the Conciergerie, the notorious prison during the Revolution (*see p. 94*)

**1356** Etienne Marcel, the merchants' provost, takes virtual control of Paris; he is murdered in 1358 by Royalists in favour of Charles V

**From 1370** Charles V begins a massive eastern fortress, soon called the Bastille (*see p. 76*), and extends the city wall begun in 1356

**1420–36** The English control Paris in alliance with the Burgundians

**1429** Joan of Arc is wounded in Paris during the Hundred Years War

**1431** Henry VI of England, aged 10, is crowned king of France in Notre-Dame Cathedral

**c. 1518** François I buys the *Mona Lisa* after Leonardo da Vinci's death (*see p. 32*)

**1572** Wedding of Protestant Henri of Navarre (future Henri IV) to Catholic Marguerite de Valois is followed by wholesale slaughter of Protestants on the eve of St Bartholomew's Day

**1578–1607** Pont Neuf, the first bridge without houses and the oldest still standing, is built

**1635** The Académie Française is founded by Cardinal Richelieu

**1686** Le Procope café established and coffee shops soon become popular meeting places (*see p. 100*)

**1751-66** Denis Diderot's *Encylopaedia* published

## The French Revolution

**1784–1791** Farmers General Wall built around Paris as a tax barrier

**1789** The Bastille stormed by mob on 14th July

**1792** Tuileries Palace attacked by mob on 10th August leading to the fall of the monarchy

**1793** Louis XVI guillotined on 21st January and Marie-Antoinette on 16th October

**1793** The Louvre becomes the Musée de la République

**1793–94** Reign of Terror during which hundreds of royalists and clerics are executed

## Napoleon and Further Revolutions

**1804** Napoleon crowns himself Emperor in Notre-Dame Cathedral

**1814** Napoleon abdicates unconditionally under Allied pressure on 6th April and the Bourbons return to power with Louis XVIII

**1828** First omnibus route opened

**1830** Suppression of liberty of the press precipitates July Revolution and abdication of Charles X

**1830** Louis-Philippe, Duc d'Orleans, becomes 'citizen king' as Roi des Français, bringing great building development to the city

**1840** Napoleon's body re-buried at Les Invalides (*see p. 119*) after his death on the island of St Helena in 1821

**1848** The Second Republic proclaimed under Napoléon III

**1852–70** Baron Haussmann transforms medieval Paris, creating 20 *arrondissements*

**1863** At the Salon des Refusés Manet's *Le Déjeuner sur l'Herbe* causes a scandal (*see p. 114*)

**1870** Napoléon III is deposed and Third Republic proclaimed

**1870–71** Franco-Prussian war results in the siege of Paris and its capitulation. A bloody insurrection follows and cruel suppression known as the Paris Commune

**1889** Inauguration of the Eiffel Tower (*see p. 111*)

## Modern Era

**1900** First Métro line opens

**1914–18** First World War puts Paris under threat

**1919** Peace conference in Paris and Treaty of Versailles signed 28th June

**1940** Marshal Pétain heads the Vichy government; Germans enter Paris

**1944** De Gaulle enters Paris on 26th August; Liberation of the city

**1946** De Gaulle resigns; Fourth Republic constitution accepted

**1958** Fifth Republic–Charles de Gaulle forms emergency government

**1968** Student riots followed by general strike; De Gaulle retires

**1970** President de Gaulle dies; Place de l'Etoile renamed Place Charles de Gaulle

**1970** RER (suburban express railway) opens

**1977** Jacques Chirac becomes first elected Mayor of Paris since 1871

**1981–95** François Mitterand is France's longest serving President

**1994** Eurotunnel opens, linking France and England under the Channel

**1995** Marie Curie becomes the first woman to be buried in the Panthéon (*see p. 94*)

**1997** Diana, Princess of Wales dies after a car crash in the city centre

**2006** First tramway inaugurated inside Paris since 1937

**2007** Nicolas Sarkozy elected President

# LOUVRE & CHAMPS-ELYSEES

# introduction

Great Parisian perspectives are nowhere more impressive than on the Right Bank of the Seine (*Rive Droit* or north of the river) where the vista stretches from the Pyramid of the Louvre, across the Tuileries and Place de la Concorde then beyond to the Champs-Elysées. This district provides ample opportunities for the insatiable culture seeker to drink deeply, but also for the *flâneur* to window gaze or chill out in cafés and gardens.

The former royal palace, the Palais du Louvre, sets the tone for grandeur and distinction and here are housed not only the extensive collections of the Musée du Louvre, but also those of the Musée des Arts Décoratifs. A short walk away, across the Tuileries Gardens, is the Musée de l'Orangerie and at the lower end of the Champs-Elysées is the Musée du Petit Palais.

Take a break from the museums to stroll along the arcaded Rue de Rivoli (*map p. 25, C1–D4*) lined with grand hotels and a variety of shops, or the parallel and older Rue St-Honoré. This lively and varied street has an old church or two, neighbourhood stores and trendy designer boutiques and passes close to the distinguished Place Vendôme. Within easy reach is the older of Paris's two opera houses, Opéra Garnier. Place de la Concorde lies between the Tuileries and the Champs-Elysées which gently ascends to the Arc de Triomphe, and more fashion houses and elegant mansions can be admired on Rue du Faubourg St-Honoré, the continuation of Rue St-Honoré.

*Page 23*: Sculpture on display inside the Musée du Louvre

# Musée du Louvre

**Open:** Wed–Mon, 9–6; Wed & Fri until 9.45pm (except public holidays) **Charges:** Entry fee except first Sun of month and 14 July **Entrances:** Main, west side of the Pyramid; others, Carrousel du Louvre, Porte des Lions-Denon Pavilion (ticket sales; closes 5.30), Passage Richelieu, ticket holders only **Tel:** 01 40 20 53 17 **Web:** www.louvre.fr **Metro:** Palais-Royal-Musée du Louvre, Louvre-Rivoli, Tuileries **Map:** p. 25, D3
**Highlights:** *Card-sharper* by Georges de la Tour; *Mona Lisa* by Leonardo da Vinci; *Barberini Ivory*; *Venus de Milo*

The Louvre is a magnificent palace containing one of the world's most diverse museums with eight huge departments. The collections are housed in three main wings, Richelieu (north), Sully (east) and Denon (south), each on four levels.

First a sombre fort, the Louvre evolved into a royal palace until it was abandoned in the 17th century by Louis XIV in favour of the palace at Versailles. On 10th August 1793 the Musée de la République was opened in the Louvre. Enriched by collections seconded from royalty, emigrants, and the Church, along with loot from Napoleon's Italian campaigns, it has remained the national art gallery and museum ever since.

Old rooms and new spaces are juxtaposed throughout the museum: the oldest surviving rooms of the palace built by Pierre Lescot for Henri II, are the Salles des Cariatides (Sully wing), the Grand Cabinet du Roi decorated c. 1660, and the Salle Henri II where the ceiling was painted by Georges Braque in 1953. The Grande Galerie along the Seine is part of the old Louvre palace built in the 16th century, and the sumptuous Apollo Gallery in the Denon wing, was decorated by Charles Le Brun for Louis XIV and revamped in the 19th century. Napoléon III built the Salle du Manège (Denon) for equestrian displays and his apartments in Richelieu can be visited.

It is almost impossible to visit the whole museum in a day. There follows a selection of the greatest pieces:

Paris

a/s/e

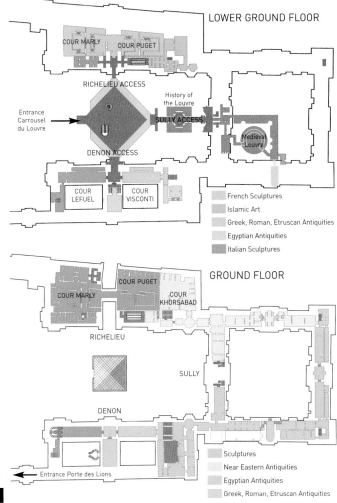

LOWER GROUND FLOOR

COUR MARLY

COUR PUGET

RICHELIEU ACCESS

History of
the Louvre

Entrance
Carrousel
du Louvre

SULLY ACCESS

Medieval
Louvre

DENON ACCESS

COUR
LEFUEL

COUR
VISCONTI

French Sculptures

Islamic Art

Greek, Roman, Etruscan Antiquities

Egyptian Antiquities

Italian Sculptures

GROUND FLOOR

COUR PUGET

COUR MARLY

COUR
KHORSABAD

RICHELIEU

SULLY

DENON

Entrance Porte des Lions

Sculptures

Near Eastern Antiquities

Egyptian Antiquities

Greek, Roman, Etruscan Antiquities

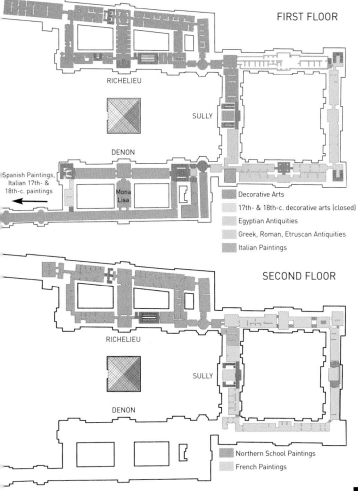

FIRST FLOOR

RICHELIEU

SULLY

DENON

Spanish Paintings,
Italian 17th- &
18th-c. paintings

Mona
Lisa

Decorative Arts

17th- & 18th-c. decorative arts (closed)

Egyptian Antiquities

Greek, Roman, Etruscan Antiquities

Italian Paintings

SECOND FLOOR

RICHELIEU

SULLY

DENON

Northern School Paintings

French Paintings

## Paintings

The huge Department of Paintings includes major collections of French, Northern and Italian Schools, and smaller collections of Spanish and English. See plan on previous page.

**French Paintings**: The department is introduced with the earliest existing French portrait, and a rare easel painting on wood, of the King, *Jean Le Bon* (c. 1350), in Room 1. The works from the School of Fontainebleau (16th century) in Rooms 9 and 10 show the influence of the Italian Renaissance on French painting, with their Mannerist elegance and allegorical rather than religious subjects. Well represented in the Louvre is Nicolas Poussin: the museum owns 38 of his canvases, a quarter of those in existence, displayed in Rooms 13, 14 and 16-19. Poussin spent much of his life in Rome, and worked out his rigorous and intellectualised compositions using miniature scenery and wax models. The richly-painted anecdotal ***Card-sharper*** (c. 1635–40) by Georges de la Tour (*see illustration opposite*), who was best known for scenes dramatically lit by candlelight, is one of only two works by him in the Louvre painted in direct light (the other is *St Thomas*). A favourite theme from Caravaggio to Cézanne, the card game provides an ideal opportunity to create a mood, study interrelationships and moralise, according to 17th century standards, on the three major temptations—gambling, wine and lust. The elegantly dressed young man on the right is being set up by companions whose body-language indicates what is about to happen, directing the viewer's focus to the card-sharper's hand on the left.

**Northern Schools**: The finely drawn *Self-Portrait* (1523) by Albrecht Dürer from Nuremberg is in Room 8. It was one of the first individual self-portraits in Western painting. Dürer holds a thistle—possibly a symbol of fidelity to his betrothed, Agnes Frey. Flemish painting in the 16th and 17th century was dominated by Peter Paul Rubens who produced a series of 24 huge, resplendent scenes of the *Life of Marie de Médicis* (1622–25), designed to decorate the Luxembourg Palace, and now displayed in Room 18. The painter's greatest single achievement, the series glorifies the life

**The *Card-sharper* by Georges de la Tour, in the Louvre French Paintings gallery**

and achievements of the Queen in an appropriately exuberant and eulogistic manner and runs in sequence from left to right, each canvas a major event of Marie's life. The *Proclamation of the Regency of the Queen* is the key moment in the cycle. In Room 31, Rembrandt's *Bathsheba Bathing* (1654) depicts the moment when Bathsheba receives the love note from King David, and was modelled by his mistress Hendrickje Stoffels.
**Italian Schools**: This collection of 13th–18th century works constitutes the oldest in the Louvre,

dating back to the reign of François I (1515–47). It also contains the museum's most famous picture, the ***Mona Lisa*** (*see box on following page*). In Room 1 *Madonna and Child in Majesty with Six Angels* (c. 1270) by Cimabue experiments with depth and naturalism; an important theme for the Florentine painters. The Venetian painters are well represented by Piero della Francesca and Giovanni Bellini. The former's intellectual style can be seen in his painting *The Portrait of Sigismondo Malatesta* (1451) in Room 4, while Bellini's

## Mona Lisa

This small portrait has tremendous power and magnetism. The Mona Lisa's gaze is benign but elusive, and seems to shift from contentment to irony, from nostalgia to self-satisfaction. The facts surrounding it are almost as mysterious. Thought to be of Mona Lisa Gherardini (correctly Monna, a variant of *mia donna*, Italian for 'my lady'), wife of a Florentine cloth merchant, Francesco di Zanobi del Giocondo. She is also called 'La Gioconda'; the word, meaning jocund in English, may provide the visual pun of the sitter's half-smile. Begun in Florence c. 1503, it is a seminal work in 16th century portrait painting. All Leonardo's experimental skills, experience and technical range are concentrated here with a naturalism not practised by his predecessors. At some point the painting was trimmed, thus creating the apparently abrupt passage from foreground to background. Both are bathed in a mutable luminosity. Crucial in obtaining the extraordinary soft tonal modelling is Leonardo's virtuoso use of *sfumato*, a natural transition between light and dark in almost imperceptible degrees achieved by applying multiple layers of glazes composed of tiny amounts of pigment to a substantial thickness of walnut-oil. The walnut-oil and oxidation account for the change in colours, which were much brighter originally. The mobility of Mona Lisa's face is enhanced further by the smudgy definition of the corners of the eyes and mouth. In contrast, hard edges such as the border of the transparent veil and the draughtsmanship displayed in her clothes, pin the image to the picture surface. One of Leonardo's favourite paintings, he took it with him when he was summoned to work for François I in Paris in 1517. After Leonardo's death, the king purchased the painting and added it to the royal collection.

**The Louvre's most famous exhibit:** *Mona Lisa* **by Leonardo da Vinci**

personal vision is developed over a number of works including *Crucifixion* (c. 1465–70) and *Virgin and Child with Saints* (c. 1487), both in Room 5. The High Renaissance (late-15th and early-16th centuries), was the moment of perfect harmony and proportion in Italian painting. In Room 7 is Titian's *The Entombment of Christ* (c. 1520), one of his greatest pictures and a highlight in this collection. It encapsulates a moment of dramatic pathos, heavy with the weight of the dead Christ and the burden of sorrow as He is carried by Pontius Pilate, St John and Nicodemus. The lighting and tone of the piece were pioneering at the time. Among the greatest artists of the era was Leonardo da Vinci, whose magnetic *Mona Lisa* is exhibited in the Salle de la Joconde (*see box on p. 32*), inside a specially protected, free-standing display case. The greatest of the Roman School artists

shown in Room 8 is Raphael. *La Belle Jardiniére* (1507) is a beautiful example of the type of Madonna which made him so famous. Caravaggio, the greatest Italian painter of the 17th century, is represented in Room 12. His *Death of the Virgin* (1605-6) was considered scandalous at the time due to the earthy realism of the figures and the dramatic contrasts of light and shade.

**Spanish Painting:** This collection is limited but includes some masterpieces, including *Young Beggar* (1650) by Murillo, *Crucifixion with Two Donors* (c. 1579) by El Greco, and *Portrait of Ferdinand Guillemardet* (1798–99) by Francisco Goya.

**English Painting** (*at present in Room 74, Sully 1st Floor, but moving to 2nd Floor by 2009*): A relatively small but high-quality collection of mainly 18th century works by masters such as Reynolds, Gainsborough, Constable, and Turner.

## Sculpture

The Louvre's collection of sculpture ranges from the Middle Ages to the mid-19th century and is dominated by French work but also includes pieces from Italy, Spain and northern Europe.

**French Sculpture:** This is organised around the courtyards of Cour Marly and Cour Puget with displays of large sculptures

designed for royal gardens or public places. The magnificent *Marly Horses* (1743–45) by Guillaume Coustou (*Richelieu* lower ground, *Cour Marly*) were commissioned for the now demolished royal Château de Marly, once the private retreat of Louis XIV. Reproductions can be seen at the end of the Champs-Elysées (*see p. 46*). In Rooms 10–19 (*Richelieu ground floor*), earlier works from the two important artistic centres of Burgundy and the Loire include the celebrated *Tomb of Philippe Pot* (1493), the Governor of Burgundy, supported by eight weepers, and a superb marble high-relief of *St George and the Dragon* (1504–9), by the talented and influential Michel Colombe. Also shown here are early 16th-century funerary monuments including the death statue of *Jeanne de Bourbon* (1521), Queen Consort of France, being gruesomely devoured by worms, and Germain Pilon's terracotta model, *Virgin of Sorrows* (c.

1580), a rare survival from a commission by Queen Catherine de Medici.

**Italian Sculpture:** Several images of the *Madonna and Child* include a delicate 15th-century terracotta by Donatello (*Denon lower ground, Room 1*). Most celebrated are Michelangelo's two unfinished *Slaves* (1513–15) in Room 4 (*Denon ground floor*). They were intended for an extravagant tomb for Pope Julius II in Rome, but for financial reasons they were passed to Henri II in 1550 before being placed in Cardinal Richelieu's collection. In the same room, high Baroque works by Gian Lorenzo Bernini include the bust of *Cardinal Richelieu* (1641), modelled on a triple portrait by Philippe de Champaigne in London, and Antonio Canova's sleekly sentimental *Cupid and Psyche* (1787–93).

## Decorative Arts

The Decorative Arts collections (*Objets d'Art*) are a vast and glittering array of artefacts, both ecclesiastical and secular, from France and other parts of Europe and span the period from the end of Antiquity to the first half of the 19th century.

**Middle Ages:** This period is represented in Rooms 1–11 (*Richelieu ground floor*). The **Barberini Ivory** from the 6th-century is the only-surviving, near-complete

leaf of an imperial diptych, and is thought to portray Emperor Justinian (527–565), and belonged to Cardinal Barberini in the 17th century. The

*Treasure of St-Denis* includes superb ornaments acquired by Suger, Abbot of St-Denis, such as *Suger's Eagle* in antique porphyry, the rock crystal *Vase of Eleanor of Aquitain* given to Louis VII by the queen, and one of the oldest pieces of French regalia, the *Coronation Sword and Scabbard*, possibly first used at the coronation of Philippe Auguste in 1179. From the Sainte-Chapelle workshop comes the ivory *Virgin and Child* (c. 1260–70), which epitomises the Gothic ideal of beauty and the skill of Parisian ivory carvers.

**Nineteenth Century**: The Apartments of Napoléon III in Rooms 82–92 (*Richelieu first floor*) are a unique ensemble of the period, with their ostentatious decor and furnishings. The Grand Salon is the largest and most sumptuous of the rooms, glittering with gold, adorned with *putti*, and draped in crimson velvet.

## Near Eastern Antiquities

Established at the Louvre in 1881, the department covers 10,000 years, ending with the advent of Islam in the 7th century. The exhibits derive from a vast mosaic of countries extending from the Indus Valley (Pakistan) to the Mediterranean.

**Room 1** (*Richelieu ground floor*): The *Pre-Cuneiform Writing Tablets* (c. 3300 BC) from Uruk IV are the first known written or inscribed clay tablets, using notches and pictograms. The *Stele of the Vultures* (2600–2330 BC), in the same room, has fragments of the oldest known historical document in the Sumerian language, from southern Mesopotamia, recording the triumphs of King Eannatum.

**Room 3** (*Richelieu ground floor*): One of the most famous exhibits here is the tall black basalt *Codex of Hammurabi* (c. 1800 BC), a complete legal and literary document covered with Akkadian text in cuneiform script which constitutes the most complete legal compendium of Antiquity.

**Room 4, Cour Khorsabad**: This area evokes the original massive scale of the great Assyrian Palace of Dur-Sharrukin, built by Sargon II (c. 721–705 BC). It contains five *lamassu*, huge winged bulls with human heads, and five plaques of the *Frieze of the Transportation of Cedar Wood* which explain that timber was carried from Lebanon by

land and by sea to Assyria.
**Room D** *(Sully ground floor)*: The *Moabite Stone*, or *Stele of Mesha* (842 BC) has a 34-line inscription recording victories over the Israelites in the reigns of Omri, Ahab and Ahaziah. This is one of the most important, if not the earliest, examples of alphabetic writing.

## Islamic Art

This is the youngest department in the Louvre and has over 1,000 works from Muslim territories extending from Spain to India, from the first centuries of the Hegira (622) to modern times.

**Rooms 8 and 9** *(Richelieu lower ground)*: The *Barberini Vase* (1237–60) was made for an Ayyubid prince (Syria) and was later presented to Pope Urban VIII (Barberini). The skillful brassworking depicts a woman in a covered litter. The *Baptistère de Saint-Louis* (c. 1320–40) is a hammered brass bowl inlaid with silver and gold, and signed six times by the craftsman Mohammed ibn al-Zain. It was first kept at the Sainte-Chapelle of the Château of Vincennes, and served as the font for the baptism of Charles XIII.

## Egyptian Antiquities

*Due to major refurbishment work the Christian (Coptic) Art collection will be closed from Spring 2008 and the Roman collection will be closed from September 2007, for two years. The Pharaonic section will remain open. Check at the information desk or online.*

**Rooms 2 and 13** *(Sully ground floor)*: The *Akhethetep mastaba* tomb provides a fascinating illustration of the life of a dignitary in Pharaonic Egypt and the depiction of his meal, complete with music and dancing. The *Crypt of Osiris* evokes the descent to the underworld of the Valley of the Kings, and preparations for the afterlife are demonstrated by mummy cases and embalming procedures.

**Rooms 22–28** *(Sully first floor)*: From the time of the great pyramids of the Old Kingdom (c. 2700–2200 BC), the *Seated Scribe* is a small, highly-coloured limestone figure with eyes of white quartz and rock crystal, from the pyramid of Didoufri, son of Cheops. The New Kingdom (c. 1550–1069 BC)

was the glorious age of the temples at Karnac and Luxor. King Akhenaton and Nefertiti (c. 1353–37 BC) left an outstanding artistic legacy. The monumental *Statue of Akhenaton* from the Colossus with an elongated head, was given to France in 1972 in thanks for saving the temples of Nubia. Among the most beautiful smaller pieces is a torso of Queen Nefertiti in red quartzite.

## Greek, Etruscan and Roman Antiquities

*Major refurbishment work in this department is due to begin in 2009. Many of the exhibits have already been or will be moved to accommodate this work. Check at the information desk or online.*

Antique art from Greece, Italy and the Mediterranean spans the origins of Hellenism (4th millennium BC) to the last days of the Roman Empire, 6th century AD. *Venus de Milo* and the *Winged Victory of Samothrace* have been highlights of the department for more than a century.

**Venus de Milo:** For over a century the *Venus de Milo* or *Aphrodite* (late 2nd century BC) has been a highlight of the Louvre collection. The statue was found accidentally by a farmer on the Aegean island of Milos in 1820, miraculously with its original head still attached. For the viewer it epitomises the nature of Ancient Greek art, with its classical face, distant gaze and hairstyle. *Venus* may have originally been holding an apple or gathering the folds of her clothes and probably stood in a temple niche.

**Winged Victory of Samothrace:** Dramatically positioned on the monumental Daru Staircase, the *Winged Victory* (late 2nd century BC) came to light in modern times on the remote Aegean island of Samothrace in 1863. It was almost certainly part of an extravagant monument erected c. 200 BC to celebrate a great Greek naval victory. The exquisite figure represents the flying divinity of victory, Nike, who alights auspiciously on the prow of a military vessel with her drapery pressed against her by the wind.

**Venus de Milo**, the epitome of Greek beauty, shown in the Louvre's Greek, Etruscan and Roman Antiquities department

# Musée des Arts Décoratifs

**Open:** Tues, Wed, Fri, 11–6; Thurs 11–9; Sat, Sun, 10–6; closed Mon
**Charges:** Entry fee, includes audioguide **Tel:** 01 44 55 57 50, **Web:**
www.lesartsdecoratifs.fr **Metro:** Palais-Royal-Louvre **Map:** p. 25, C2
**Highlights:** candelabra by Duvuvier; apartment of Jeanne Lanvin

The Decorative Arts Museum, in the Pavillon Marsan and Rohan wing of the Louvre Palace, is totally autonomous from the Louvre Museum. The building itself is stunning, arranged around an oval atrium with a glass roof. The outstanding decorative and ornamental works of art on display are a unique account of the French way of life from medieval times to the present.

**Middle Ages to Eighteenth century** (*3rd Floor, Rooms 1–18*): The earliest 'Period Room' is a late 15th-century chamber with a canopied bed, a fireplace, wood panelling and a five-part tapestry entitled the *Romance of the Rose* (c. 1420) representing courtly life. The later collections concentrate on the new ornamental vocabulary which emerged with the development of cabinet-making, and sophisticated marquetry techniques fashionable in Paris. An example of innovative furniture design by Northern European craftsmen is the *Cupboard with Seven Columns* (1715–20) from Strasbourg. **Eighteenth Century** (*4th Floor, Rooms 19–30*): Two fashions which took hold in Europe in this period were Rococo, inspired by water, pebbles and shells, and Chinoiserie which was influenced by Chinese lacquered decoration. The extraordinary versatility and reinvention of Rococo, which could transform an object, is aptly demonstrated by a swirling **candelabra by Duvuvier**, produced 1734–35, and a sauceboat in Vincennes porcelain (1756) by Duplessis. Among objects in the Lacquered Room (c. 1770) is a little desk which belonged to Madame de Pompadour, with a blue lacquer. A remarkable clock belonging to Marie-Antoinette is from the later part of the century when Classical sources, particularly

**The Art Deco apartment of the French couturier Jeanne Lanvin, in the Musée des Arts Décoratifs (see following page)**

Etruscan, were influential.
**Nineteenth century** (*4th floor, Rooms 31–42*)**:** In the search for ideal beauty, artists turned to Antiquity for inspiration and the Empire Style was born. Typical is the beautiful Directoire chair (1795–99) by Jacob Frères. The single-minded Duchesse de Berry was a resident of these rooms in the 1820s. Her husband, the Duke of Bordeaux, was assassinated in 1820, and their son, '*l'enfant du miracle*' and successor to the Bourbon line, was born soon after. Her son's grand ceremonial cradle is shown here.

The Duchesse was involved in a plot to restore the Bourbons to the throne but was imprisoned in 1832.
**Art Nouveau** (*4th floor, Rooms 43–49*)**:** This popular section includes a 'Period Room' conceived by Georges Hoentschell for the Universal Exhibition in 1900, with original textiles. Also on display are objects by School of Nancy master craftsmen such as the glassmaker Emile Gallé, and cabinetmakers Louis Majorelle and Victor Prouvé. Hector Guimard, who was responsible for the Métro

entrances, is represented with furniture he designed for the industrialist Léon Nozal.

**Art Deco** (*3rd floor, Rooms 50–53*): Here are three complete rooms (1921–24) from the **apartment of Jeanne Lanvin**, a French couturier, by Armand-Albert Rateau, which incorporate a very personal taste in accessories; a more restrained and sombre design for a dining room (1920–21) by Louis Süe; and the innovative Ambassador's Office (1925), designed by the leading designers of the time, with domed ceiling by Pierre Chareau, a rug by Jean Lurçat and sculpture by Jacques Lipchitz.

**1940s to 2000** (*9th floor–5th floor*): This unique section was rebuilt in metal and glass in 1873, and offers magnificent views over the Jardins des Tuileries. The exhibits are varied, and sometimes amusing and a highlight is the 1960s display where the chair reigns supreme. Around 100 examples are shown including designs by Niki de Saint Phalle, who designed the fountain outside the Pompidou Centre (*see p. 64*). Not to be missed is a range of contemporary chairs from which to watch film clips featuring iconic modern furniture.

# Musée du Petit Palais

**Open:** Tues–Sun, 10–6; Tues, during temporary exhibitions, 10–8; closed Mon **Charges:** Free entry, permanent collections; entry fee, temporary exhibitions **Tel:** 01 53 43 40 00 **Web:** www.petitpalais. paris.fr **Disabled access:** Ground level to right of main entrance, and tactile visit for visually impaired **Metro:** Champs-Elysées Clemeceau **Map:** p. 24, D3
**Highlights:** *Vase Cypripedium* by Emile Gallé; *Girls on the Banks of the Seine* by Gustave Courbet

The Musée des Beaux-Arts de la Ville de Paris (Fine Arts Museum of the City of Paris) opened in 1902 in the Petit Palais. Its grandiose neo-classical façade belies the 'modern' aspect of the building, which used cast iron, concrete and glass in its reconstruction. The collec-

**Gustave Courbet's detailed observations are captured in his *Girls on the Banks of the Seine*, in the Musée du Petit Plais**

tions, acquired through purchases, commissions and donations, have resulted in a rather curious mix of art, antiquities and icons.

The First Floor contains art and artefacts from the late 19th century and Paris in 1900, including a unique piece by Emile Gallé, an Art Nouveau glass-maker from Nancy, the **Vase Cypripedium** (1898) which was inspired by the *Sabot-de-Venus* (Lady's Slipper) wild orchid and is a pioneering example of the complicated procedure of glass marquetry. Finely executed Realist paintings in the collection include two major works by Courbet, **Girls on the Banks of the Seine** (1857; *see above*) and *Sleep* (1866). The figures in both paintings are beautifully observed, a skill thought to have been influenced by the developing trend for photography. Portable painting equipment on display testifies to the practicalities essential for *plein air* painting of the

Impressionist Movement. Monet's *Sunset at Lavacourt* (1880), painted outdoors at the moment when ice on the river was melting, is a masterful example. Ambroise Vollard, art dealer and supporter of avant-garde artists, was a popular subject, painted by Cézanne in 1899, Renoir c. 1911 and Bonnard c. 1924. In 1899 Henri Matisse purchased Cézanne's *Three Bathers* (c. 1879–82) from Vollard. He kept it for 36 years, until he donated it to the Petit Palais, when he wrote: '...*it has provided me with moral support in critical moments in my adventure as an artist; I have drawn from it my faith and my perseverance...*'. In stark contrast are examples of 18th-century decorative arts, including a beautiful Sedan Chair (c. 1700), and an elaborate clock with a metal and porcelain case, *The Orchestra of Monkeys*, from Germany. A handsome wrought-iron balustrade embellishes stairs to the Ground Floor.

On the Ground Floor are examples of Romantic and Classic 19th-century work. *Roman Oldalisque* (1843) is a beautifully balanced nude by Corot, and Manet's painting of the dandified Cognac merchant, journalist and art critic, *Théodore Duret* (1868), includes an impeccable still-life. Bartholomé's *femme fatale*, landscapes by Ménard and Brokman, experimental works by Henry Cros, and pastels by Odilon Redon illustrate the range and mysteries of Symbolism, captured also in the sinuous lines of Hector Guimard's dining room, and superb jewellery by Georges Fouquet. Romantic nostalgia includes an imagined scene by Ingres, *François I at The Death of Leonardo da Vinci* (1818). Among some quality 17th-century Dutch and Flemish works, Rembrandt's *Self-Portrait in Oriental Costume* (1631) cuts a striking dash. French works of the period include Claude Lorrain's *Landscape with the Port of Santa Marinella* (1637–38), and a warm-toned still life by Nicolas de Largillierre, *Red Partridge in a Niche*. Among precious Renaissance objects are timepieces from France and northern Europe, such as three pieces of St-Porchaire ceramics which were always too fragile to be of any practical use. In the Egyptian and Classical Antiquities collection are an outstanding white-ground Greek ceramic vase attributed to Psiax (c. 525 bc), and the Roman silver dish, *Esquilin Patera* (c. 380). There is a section devoted to Universal Expositions which were so important in promoting artistic innovations in Paris.

# in the area

**Arc de Triomphe** (*open daily April–Sept 9.30am–11pm; Oct–March, 10am–11.30pm, closed 1 Jan, 1 May, 14 July, 25 Dec, 8 May, 11 Nov, entry fee, Metro: Charles de Gaulle Étoile*). High and mighty at the top of the Champs-Elysées the Arc de Triomphe reigns over the traffic chaos of Place Général de Gaulle. First envisaged by Napoleon, the largest triumphal arch in the world (almost 50m high and 45m wide) was completed in 1836. The funeral cortège bearing Napoleon's ashes passed under it in 1840. The tomb of the Unknown Soldier is beneath the Arch, and on its façades are colossal relief carvings, the most dynamic being François Rude's *La Marseillaise*. From the top of the Arch are giddy views along the Champs-Elysées and Avenue de la Grande Armée. **Map p. 24, B1**

**Arc de Triomphe, Napoleon's triumphal arch, is the largest in the world**

**Champs-Elysées** (*Metro: Champs-Élysées Clemenceau, Franklin D Roosevelt*). Emulated by many city planners, the most famous of avenues gently ascends to the northwest from Place de la Concorde to the Arc de Triomphe for nearly 2km. In 1670 marshland was drained and laid out to designs by Le Nôtre to create a promenade in the same perspective as the Tuileries Gardens. It acquired the name Champs-Elysées later when it was replanted and extended, but it was only in the mid-19th century that mansions and hotels were built and it became fashionable. Parisians and visitors still flock to it, although time has taken its toll on the Elysian Fields and its former elegance is a little faded. There are pleasant gardens at the lower end, and it is particularly alluring at night with lights in the trees. **Map p. 24, B1–D4**

**Musée Guimet**, Musée National des Arts Asiatiques (*open Wed–Mon, 10–6, entry fee except 1st Sun of month, Tel: 01 56 52 53 00, www.museeguimet.fr, Metro: Iéna*). Musée Guimet is the most important museum of Asian arts in France, its outstanding collections illustrate the diversity of cultures and civilisations throughout Asia. Named after Emile Guimet, a 19th century industrialist with a passion for ancient religions and Asian art, his collections were transferred here in 1889. Indian sculptures span a period from the 3rd millennium BC to the 19th century, and among some of the oldest pieces are the beautiful Amaravati School marble Head of Buddha (2nd century) and a Buddha torso (early 6th century) from the Gupta period dressed in fine monastic robes. The Southeast Asian section has some of the most beautiful Khmer sculptures outside Cambodia, including the Bantah Srei Pediment (c. 967) a high-relief carving of Krishna in an animated struggle during an episode from the Mahabharata. One of the museum's great treasures is the largest collection of Gandhara sculpture (mainly 2nd and 3rd centuries AD) in the West, a style born of a remarkable union between Buddhist, Ancient Greek and Roman art in the valleys of the Hindu Kush, Afghanistan. The huge China section has exceptionally beautiful terracotta *mingqi*, funerary statuettes, from the Han and Northern Wei dynasties (206 BC–589AD), but even more graceful are Tang dynasty *sancai* figurines of dancers and courtiers (618–907). There are outstanding examples of three-coloured ceramic ware (yellow, green and white glazes) developed by Tang potters, and the rare Yuan dynasty porcelain Meiping vase. Enamels and the *cloisonné* technique are spectacularly employed in the *Vase of a Thousand Flowers* (18th century). There are also some 1,000 paintings, including the Yuan-period scroll *Bamboo* (1279–1368), a superb demonstration of the perfectly controlled use of tones of black. The Japanese department includes ceramics, funerary objects, austere ink paintings and Raku Tea Bowls. Kyoto was the artistic centre in the 17th century, but was overtaken by Edo, famous for *ukiyo-e* coloured wood-block prints by artists such as Utamaro, Hokusai and Hiroshige. **Map p. 24, D1**

**Musée de l'Orangerie** (*open Wed–Mon, 12.30–7, Fri 12.30–9, closed Tues, entry fee, Tel: 01 44 77 80 07, Metro: Concorde*) This small gallery is best known for Monet's sensational series of *Waterlilies* (*Nymphéas; 1914–26*), occupying two purpose-built rooms. The eight compositions transform the walls of the galleries into the lily ponds of Monet's gardens at Giverny, drenched in colour and reflected light, an all-encompassing experience. In the lower-ground galleries is an eclectic group which includes characteristic paintings by Renoir of young girls at the piano, fourteen wonderful works by Cézanne, and Blue and Pink-Period paintings by Picasso alongside examples of Matisse's decorative Nice paintings of the 1920s. More unusual are the largest group of works in France by Henri 'Le Douanier' Rousseau, which include *Père Junier's Cart* (1910); a number of the apparently 'simplified' portraits by Amadeo Modigliani, and examples of whimsical works by his lover, Marie Laurencin. Also, 1920–30s compositions by André Derain, which show a shift to solemn post-war realism, the desolate townscapes of Maurice Utrillo, alcoholic son of Suzanne Valladon, and disturbing, impasto Expressionist works of Chaïm Soutine. **Map p. 25, C1**

**Opéra Garnier** (*foyers, museum and auditorium open daily 10–5, tickets Mon–Sat, 10.30–6.30, closed Sun pm, 1 Jan, 1 May, entry fee, Tel: 01 40 01 22 63, Metro: Opéra*). An appropriately lavish monument to the grandiose period of the Second Empire, built 1861–75 from Charles Garnier's designs, it faces down Avenue de l'Opéra. The façade, flanked by a flight of steps, is adorned with coloured marbles and allegorical groups, including (right) *The Dance* by Jean-Baptiste Carpeaux (original in the Musée d'Orsay; *see p. 112*). Inside are the marble and onyx Grand Staircase and elaborate chandeliers. The auditorium is resplendent in red plush and gilt, and has five tiers of boxes. The dome, in disturbing contrast to the décor, was painted with murals in 1964 by Marc Chagall. The charming museum has exhibitions selected from its vast collections. **Map p. 25, A2**

**Place de la Concorde** (*Metro: Concorde*). A beautiful open space next to the Seine designed by Jacques-Ange Gabriel as a monument to Louis XV, with colonnaded 18th-century mansions on the north side. The *Obelisk of Luxor*, originally from a temple in Upper Egypt, was presented to the king,

Louis-Philippe, in 1831. In the mid-18th century the empty site was chosen to receive a bronze statue of Louis XV, and the *Marly Horses* (replicas, originals in the Musée du Louvre; *see p. 34*) at the entrance to the Champs-Elysées were installed later. Renamed Place de la Révolution in 1792, a huge figure of *Liberty* replaced Louis XV's statue, and it became the bloody arena of executions. On 21st January 1793, Louis XVI fell to the guillotine blade, which claimed 1,119 victims. It acquired its present name in 1795, was renamed Place Louis XV in 1815, and reverted to Concorde in 1830. **Map p. 25, C1**

**St-Eustache** (*open 9–7 Mon–Sat, 8.15–12.30 & 2.30–7 Sun, free entry, Metro: Les Halles*). This handsome church standing on the edge of Les Halles, with a mixture of Gothic, Renaissance and neo-classical design, was built 1532–1788. Molière was baptised in St-Eustache and, always noted for its music, this was where Berlioz conducted the first performance of his *Te Deum* (1855) and Liszt his *Messe Solenelle* (1866). The Musicians' Chapel on the south commemorates Rameau, Franz Liszt and Mozart's mother, whose funeral was held here in 1778. The organ, one of the most important in Paris, has an ornate case by Victor Baltard (1854), architect of Les Halles. Among outstanding works are the incomplete tomb of Colbert (d. 1683), designed by Le Brun, with statues of *Colbert and Fidelity* by Antoine Coysevox and by J. B. Tuby, and on the altar of the Lady Chapel is a *Virgin* by J.-B. Pigalle. The stained glass featuring St Anthony was given by the Société de la Charcuterie de France—the pig being one of the saint's attributes. **Map p. 25, C4**

**St Germain l'Auxerrois** (*open daily 8–7, free entry, Tel: 01 42 60 13 96, Metro: Louvre Rivoli*). The former parish church of the Louvre Palace, stands on the site of a Merovingian sanctuary. The conspicuous neo-Gothic north tower is 19th century. Inside, 18th-century classicism mingles with Gothic. The main attraction is the royal pew (1682–84), a *tour-de-force* of wood carving, by Charles Le Brun and François Mercier. The wood is worked to represent a draped canopy above fretwork panels and supported by Ionic columns. There is also an 18th-century *Christ* carved in wood by Edmé Bouchardon. The oldest part of the church is the base of the belfry (12th century). On 24th August 1572, the church bell, *la Marie*, signalled the start of the Massacre of St Bartholomew, the wholesale slaughter of Huguenots. **Map p. 25, D3**

**Ornate decorations in Place de la Concorde, designed by Jacques-Ange Gabriel in the 18th century as a monument to Louis XV**

## Gardens of Paris

One of Europe's greenest capitals, Paris has an array of gardens which offer a calm alternative to the shopping, eating and sightseeing in the city. Not only places to seek shade and solitude, Paris's green spaces are historical centres and informal art galleries. The **Jardins du Palais Royal** (*Metro: Palais Royal; Map p. 25, C3*) is an oasis of lime trees and flowerbeds, with arcaded buildings on three sides. The houses were a speculative venture in 1781–86 and it became a fashionable place to be seen, and smart restaurants were opened such as Le Grand Véfour (*see page opposite*). Here, on 13th July 1789, Camille Desmoulins delivered the fiery harangue which precipitated the fall of the Bastille, and Charlotte Corday purchased the knife to kill the anti-Royalist Marat. Twentieth-century residents included the effete, multi-talented Jean Cocteau and earthy female writer Colette. The **Jardin des Tuileries** (*Metro: Tuileries; Map p. 25, C1–C2*) were named after the medieval tile-kilns (*tuileries*), sited here from the 12th century. It is the oldest garden in Paris, developed in the 16th century, and the first public garden. Covering 32 hectares, it has three distinct parts: formal gardens with the Round Pond; the Grand Couvert, a wooded central area; and the large Octagon pond. Since the 18th century the garden has been enlivened with over 100 statues, among them 18 bronzes by Maillol, and works by Giacometti, Max Ernst and Jean Dubuffet. **Jardin du Luxembourg** (*RER: Luxembourg; Map p. 84, C1–D2*) surrounds the Palais du Luxembourg and is less formal and more varied than the Tuileries, embellished by over 80 statues, two fountains and a pond. Planned in the 17th century for Marie de Médicis, today there are cafés, a bandstand, carousel, marionette theatre, and chess-players locked in combat. Among the statues are a replica of Bartoldi's *Statue of Liberty* given to the United States in 1885, *Stendhal* by Rodin and a monument to Eugène Delacroix by Dalou.

# eat

There is no scarcity of places to eat in the immediate area of the Louvre (**map p. 25, D3**). Along Rue St-Honoré are some of the newer, fashionable restaurants such as Costes (*see below*), and the large Place du Marché-St-Honoré, dominated by Ricardo Bofill's modern, glass construction, is lined with cheerful cafés and restaurants. Palais Royal is also a pleasant alternative, especially in summer, where restaurants of every category reside under the surrounding arcades and adjacent streets, including Le Grand Véfour (*see below*). For price categories, see p. 12.

**1 €€€€ Le Grand Véfour**, *17 Rue de Beaujolais, Tel: 01 42 96 56 27, open Mon–Thur 12.30–1.30pm, 8–9.30pm, Fri 12.30–2, closed Sat, Sun, Christmas, Easter, August, Metro: Palais Royal.* Under the arcades of the Palais Royal, this is one of the city's oldest and greatest restaurants, and has been popular with everyone from Napoleon Bonaparte to Jean Cocteau. It still attracts the great and the good, who come to revel in the delights of chef Guy Martin's two-star Michelin cooking which goes from strength to strength. The choices range from classic to very adventurous *haute cuisine*. One of his most celebrated dishes is *raviolis de foie-gras à l'emulsion de crème truffée* and an unusual dessert is the *tourte aux artichauts*, a recipe from the chef's native Savoy. In addition to the setting, an 18th-century building with mirrors, painted panels and chandeliers, is the pleasure derived from the impeccable but not intimidating service. The kitchens, cellars and cigar reserve may be visited.
Map p. 25, C3

**2 €€€ Café Costes**, *Hôtel Costes, 239 Rue St-Honore, Tel: 01 42 44 50 00, open until 4am, Metro: Tuileries.* Close to Place Vendôme, in a very prestigious area, dimly lit rooms bring an air of intimacy and mystery to the classy Hôtel Costes. A long, narrow entrance opens onto a beautiful square patio open to the sky with terracotta walls, overlooked by a loggia and statues wreathed in ivy. Around the patio are small, intimate dining areas and at the back of the ground floor, a bar. Described as the place to see the beautiful people of Paris, it is the young and sexy waiters and waitresses (length of leg evidently the main requisite) who are the real hot numbers although the service can take a while to warm up, but when it does it's excellent. The fusion cuisine is attractively varied and excellently cooked although, in true Costes style, the choices are quite limited. You can dally with a Club Sandwich or indulge in lobster and caviar, and desserts range from trifle to carpaccio of ginger. Summer choices include a delicate dish of lightly cooked, crunchy *haricot verts* to start, and a succulent *thiou tigre qui pleure*, sliced beef with the slightly spiced sauce served separately. **Map p. 25, B2**

**③ €€ Angl'Opéra**, ■ *39 Avenue de l'Opéra, Tel: 01 42 61 86 25, open Mon–Fri, noon–11, Metro: Opéra*. An attractive and comfortable corner restaurant in the Edouard VII Hotel (*see p. 15*), close to the Opéra, where the cuisine has been described as iconoclastic. The chef, Gille Choukroun, is famous for his interesting—even outrageous—combinations of ingredients and flavours, where scallops sprinkled with chocolate are really quite acceptable. The limited-selection menu changes regularly and it takes a while to tune into the descriptions which, conversely, guard the name of the key ingredient until the end: *crème brulee*, green radish, soya sauce....and foie gras; or grilled grapefruit, green tea, spinach...and rumpsteak. The presentation is stunning and eating here is a fascinating experience. Meals are also served in the bar and on the terrace. **Map p. 25, B2**

**④ €€ Flora**, *36 Avenue George V, Tel: 01 40 70 10 49, closed Sat lunch, Sun. Metro: George V.* Modern, sleek and sexy, the restaurant is named after owner/chef, Flora Mikula, who grew up in Avignon and opened her first restaurant Les Olivades in 1996. In 2002 she moved on, and while the Provençal influences are still there, she went for a more sophisticated blend taking inspiration from world cooking, especially Thai. She uses fresh vegetables and fruit in season, especially aubergine, mushrooms and truffles, which are colourfully combined with seafood, langoustines, lobster or scallops, or delicate lamb or veal. Excellent desserts include pink grapefruit and oranges with hibiscus syrup, chocolaty things, and even roast figs with cheesy ice cream. **Map p. 24, C2**

**⑤ €€ Macéo**, ■ *15 Rue des Petits-Champs, Tel: 01 42 97 53 85, open noon–2.30, 7.30–11, Metro: Bourse, Pyramides.* A chic yet traditional address in a coolly beautiful setting, near the Bibliothèque Richelieu (National Library), where the service is impeccable. The décor is period-piece combined with curious modern fittings, and the space is divided between the bar area, which can seat 20 and serves light meals, and the main dining room, Salle Palais Royal, with large windows and a tiny library corner with a couple of tables. Upstairs is the Second-Empire Salle de Bal. The owner,

Englishman Marc Williamson (proprietor of Willi's Wine Bar along the street; *see p. 55*), takes care of the wine selection, and the reputation of chef Thierry Bourbonnais goes before him. The cooking is extremely fine and stylish but not overly elaborate. The choices change with the seasons and the market, and includes a *menu vert* (vegetarian) and *menu decouverte*, of 3 courses (with two choices on each). The summertime *menu asperge* is four heavenly courses incorporating the green, white and purple spikes in one way or another —probably not in the dessert. A

nice touch is butter served with the bread. **Map p. 25, C3**

**6** **€€ Café Marly**, *93 Rue de Rivoli, Cour Napoleon, Musée du Louvre, Tel: 01 49 26 06 60, open daily 8–2am, Metro: Palais Royal.* This Costes classic in the Richelieu wing of the Louvre is a very popular watering hole and a convenient place to eat during a visit to the museum. Overlooking Cour Napoleon and the Pyramid du Louvre, in fine weather tables are set out on the arcaded terrace. Inside there is a view onto part of the Louvre's 19th century French sculpture collection in Cour Marly. Fun, fashionable and

**The fashionable and bustling Café Marly has an enviable view out to Ieoh Ming Pei's Louvre Pyramid at the Musée du Louvre**

bustling, the setting and the décor account in major part for its popularity. The menu is fairly simple—a club sandwich or a main course—with a small choice, but the cooking is reliable. **Map p. 25, D3**

⑦ **€€ Le Saut du Loup**, *Musée des Art Décoratifs, 107 Rue de Rivoli, Tel: 01 42 25 49 55, open daily, noon–2am, Metro: Tuileries.* Accessed from the entrance hall, it has a unique location overlooking the Carrousel gardens, on two levels with a large terrace. The interior, designed by Philippe Boisseilier, has been kept deliberately low-key to avoid competing with the setting and the tables have been arranged so that the view can be appreciated by every customer. Chef Pascal Bernier has, as is the fashion, created a menu which offers a range of good ingredients served simply but imaginatively, such as *foie-gras poëlé* with orange, old-fashioned vegetables with truffles, and a 'liquid' chocolate cake with almond-milk ice-cream. It is open for lunch, tea and dinner. **Map p. 25, C2**

⑧ **€€ Le Soufflé**, *36 Rue du Mont-Thabor, Tel: 01 42 60 27 19, open daily noon–2.30, 7–10, closed part of Feb, Aug, Metro: Concorde.* Tucked away in a corner, close to the Tuileries Gardens and Place de la Concorde, this much-loved restaurant has been here for an eternity, and reassuringly hasn't changed a great deal. With just two smallish dining areas, it is the *soufflé* centre of Paris. *Soufflés* come in every flavour, and it is possible to have

one for every course. But there are alternatives, with meatier and crunchier dishes on offer. The pièce de résistance is *soufflé au Grand Marnier*, a dish which induces nostalgia for the 60s when it was *the dessert* in all the best restaurants; now it is quite rare. Crisp on the outside, slightly liquid in the middle, and *arosé* with the alcohol. Utter heaven! **Map p. 25, B2**

⑨ **€ Le Fumoir**, *Rue de l'Amiral Coligny, Tel: 01 42 92 00 24, open daily 11–2am, Metro: Louvre Rivoli.* The slightly sombre interior, where people take relaxing seriously, combines bar, restaurant and library with comfortable chairs and it attracts young, confident customers. Sophisticated cocktails are mixed at the antique American bar, yet the Fumoir has a lived-in atmosphere, especially in winter; in summer there are tables outside on the pavement terrace. Immediately behind the Louvre, next to the Church of St-Germain-l'Auxerrois, it is well positioned for lunch after a morning of culture-bashing, or a *café glacé* at the end of the afternoon. The food is modern, reliable and easy on the wallet. **Map p. 25, D3**

⑩ **The White Bar**, *15 Avenue Montaigne, Tel: 01 47 23 55 99. Metro: Alma Marceau.* In one of the most chic and fashionable avenues in town, off the Champs-Elysées, this is the new in-place. The Mezzanine bar of the Maison Blanche restaurant, Philippe Starck-inspired, has luxurious white Italian sofas, black and white photos, a phosphorescent bar which changes colour, smart cocktails and trendy snacks. The terrace is 7 floors up, on the roof of the Theatre des Champs-Elysées, in the shadow of the Eiffel Tower. **Map p. 24, D2**

**11 Willy's Wine Bar**, *13 Rue des Petits-Champs, Tel: 01 42 61 05 09. M: Bourse.* Opened by Englishman Mark Williamson in 1980, this was the first wine bar in Paris, and continues to be enormously successful, with around 250 wines on the list. In a 1930s building, the bar has a great ambiance and a *dégustation* may be accompanied by a meal cooked by gifted chef, François Yon, using fresh ingredients with a Mediterranean slant. The back room features a collection of Willy's Wine Bar posters. **Map p. 25, C3**

---

### Time for tea

To help you revive after a heavy day of culture and shopping, there are several elegant tea rooms in the area, such as **Angelina's** (*222 Rue de Rivoli, map p. 25, C2*) where you can indulge in a rich hot chocolate or a *mont blanc* made from *crème de marron*. The elegant department store, **Printemps** (*see illustration below, and p. 59*) has a tearoom on Level 6. **Ladurée** (*16 Rue Royale, map p. 25, B1*), founded in 1862 and famous for its macaroons, is open every day; and **Fauchon's** (*24–30 Place de la Madeleine, map p. 25, B1*), the exclusive grocery shop since 1895, was followed by a *salon de thé* in 1898.

Another **Ladurée** restaurant/tea room and patisserie (*75 Avenue des Champs-Elysees, map p. 24, C2*) is open every day. Close to Palais Royal is **A Priori Thé**, (*35–37 Galerie Vivienne, map p. 25, B3*) which makes a pleasant break for a light lunch or tea in the old shopping arcade.

# shop

Classy boutiques dominate this area, along Rue St-Honoré and its continuation to the west, Rue du Faubourg St-Honoré, culminating with *haute couture* houses on Avenue Matignon (*map p. 24, C3–B3*). Delicatessens jostle with smart boutiques and chocolatiers with expensive jewellers in this part of town. A good refuge on a wet day is the Forum des Halles, a vast three-level below-ground shopping precinct with direct access from the metro/RER (*map p. 25, D4*) Here, there is a large Fnac store, numerous clothing chains and the Forum des Créateurs for young designers (*Metro: Les Halles/RER: Châtelet Les Halles*).

## RUE ST-HONORE AND VICINITY

**Chanel**, *29–31 Rue Cambon, Tel: 01 42 86 26 00, Metro: Madeleine.* This is a remarkable story of enduring stylishness. Coco Chanel, born Gabrielle Bonheur Chanel in 1883, set up shop, and home, at no. 21 Rue Cambon in 1910 and began her millinery empire. The key to her success was the classic simplicity of her little black dress, the quilted bag, and, of course, Chanel No. 5 perfume. A downturn during World War II saw her popularity diminish because of an affair with a Nazi officer and an exile of sorts to Switzerland, but after her come-back in 1945 her designs became all the rage, and included pea jackets and bell-bottoms for women. She worked to the very end and her ideas are now cleverly reinvented by Karl Lagerfeld. **Map p. 25, B2**

**Michel Cluizel (La Fontaine au Chocolat)**, *201 Rue St-Honoré, Tel: 01 42 44 11 66, Metro: Tuileries, Palais Royal.* Michel Cluizel, *chocolatier par excellence*, has been making chocolate since 1948 and his family carries on the tradition. Michel scours the globe for outstanding cocoa plantations and his products contain only pure ingredients. His mouth-watering range, produced in workshops in Normandy, includes *Les 1ers Crus des Plantations*, which uses the highest quality cocoa beans, and should be *dégusté* in the same way as fine wine; a range of milk and plain chocolate bars, *Les Grandes Teneurs en Cacao*, which includes *Noir Infini* with 99% cocoa; and a selection of bonbons called the *Lilliputiens*. **Map p. 25, C2**

**Colette**, *213 Rue St-Honoré, Tel: 01 55 35 33 90, Metro: Tuileries.* This trendiest of concept stores is described as a 'progressive boutique'. Off-beat and eclectic, it is named after its owner who carefully selects the items by drawing on all types of culture, or sub-culture, and has maintained this standard since opening in 1997. Colette is abreast of every fashion tropism, fad or novelty—present and future—and stocks everything that the fashion conscious woman or man might need...and even what they don't know they need. There is clothing by Dolce & Gabbana, Marni, Miu Miu, and a range of designer fashion items from mobile-phone accessories, to Icelandic soap. Colette has a finger on the pulse of music, the arts, and design. The boutique's further claim to fame is the slick café and water-bar in the *sous-sol* which carries an infinite choice of bottled waters and mainly veggie food. **Map p. 25, C2**

**Dehillerin**, *18–20 Rue Coquillière, Tel: 01 42 36 53 13, Metro: Les Halles, Louvre.* The reassuringly old-fashioned shop-front is a clue to the seriousness of this store which has been equipping Parisian kitchens since 1820. There's nothing the Dehillerin family doesn't know about kitchen hardware. The exhaustive range of *batterie de cuisine*, enough to send cooks delirious, is stacked, displayed, and suspended from every surface. To inspire culinary achievement are devices such as huge copper pans, tiny moulds for chocolates, best-ever chopping boards, mollusc forks, duck presses and apple peelers. **Map p. 25, C3–C4**

**John Galliano**, *384–386 Rue St-Honoré, Tel: 01 55 35 40 40, Metro: Madeleine.* Everything about Galliano designs is outrageous and spectacular, including the all-glass boutique designed by Michel Wilmotte which is worth the detour. The effect stuns and destabilises, and colourful ready-to-wear fashions including shoes, lingerie and beachwear are set off to full effect. Flamboyant eye candy decoration and jokiness add to the originality of the place on all levels, including the loos. Delighting in colour, specialising in deconstruction, wit and magic, Galliano is one of the most influential fashion designers of our time. **Map p. 25, B1**

**Christian Louboutin**, *19 Rue Jean-Jacques Rousseau, Tel: 01 42 36 05 31, Metro: Louvre-Rivoli.* The fantastic and fabulous shoes of Christian Louboutin have to be mentioned. Elegant, witty, sexy, outrageous, they might be trimmed with satin or crystal beads or have a beer-can heel, and always have red soles. Humour and whimsicality is teamed with hand-finished care and remarkable comfort even if the heels are startlingly high. Sought after by international stars, they are incredibly expensive. **Map p. 25, D3–C3**

a/s/e | Paris

**Marcel Marongiu**, *203 Rue St-Honoré, Tel: 01 49 27 96 38, Metro: Tuileries.* One of France's most popular designers manages successfully to blend sophistication and practicality. Marongiu introduces artistic influences into his creations, particularly the effects of colour or non-colour from painters as wide ranging as van Dyck and Rothko. His Franco/Swedish background ensures there is an interesting balance between innovation and wearability. **Map p. 25, C2**

## GRANDS MAGASINS

Directly behind Opéra Garnier, on Boulevard Haussmann, are two legendary department stores, **Printemps** and **Galeries Lafayette** (*map p. 25, A1–A3*). A visit to one or both is a complete day out in paradise for the shopaholic.

**Galeries Lafayette**, *40 Boulevard Haussmann, Tel: 01 42 82 34 56, open Mon–Sat 9.30–7.30, Thurs 9.30–9. Metro: Chaussée-d'Antin.* This famous and elegant emporium has three stores. Lafayette Coupole, which extends over seven floors includes three tiers of balconies covered with a glazed dome (1912) and boasts the largest women's fashion choice in the world, with a breathtaking 75,000 labels (Levels 1, 2 and 3). Lafayette Homme, for men, covers three floors, including Gourmet Food and Wine on Level 1, and Lafayette Maison has three levels. There are places to eat on almost every floor, among them on Level 6, the self-service Lafayette Caffe overlooking Paris. Fashion shows on Level 7, Friday at 3, must be booked: welcome@ galeries-lafayette. com, Tel: 01 42 82 36 40.

**Printemps**, *64 Boulevard Haussmann, Tel: 01 42 82 50 00, open Mon–Sat 9.35–7, Thurs 9.35–10. Metro: Hauvre-Caumartin.* The multitude of departments are divided between three stores: de la Mode, de la Maison and de l'Homme. Fashion and accessories cover 3,000m square in the Mode store, a magnificent building of 1889, including departments for teenagers and children. Under the cupola on Level 6 are a restaurant and tearoom. On Level 9 is La Terrasse restaurant, with a 360º panoramic view. For men, there is every type of clothing, from city-suits to trendy outfits in the 7-floor Printemps de l'Homme where, on Level 5 is the World Bar. For personal shopping advice, make an appointment, Tel: 01 42 82 66 11.

**An extravagant window display from Paris's premier shopping emporium, Galeries Lafayette on Boulevard Haussmann**

## RUE DU FAUBOURG ST-HONORE

Rue du Faubourg St-Honoré (*map p. 24, A2–C4*), became fashionable in the early 18th century, and its grand mansions include the Elysées Palace, official residence of the French President. One of the most chic streets in Paris, the route to Avenue Matignon is a window-gazing haze of fashion houses, designer boutiques and jewellers.

You'll find a delicious range of colourful handbags chez **Renaud Pellegrin** at no. 14 (*Tel: 01 45 48 36 30*); **Chanel** accessories at no. 21 (*Tel: 01 53 05 98 95*); the timeless silk squares and luxury leather accessories and perfumes at **Hermès** original shop, no. 24 (*Tel: 01 40 17 47 17*); **Chloë**, at 54–56 (*Tel: 01 44 94 33 00*), selling the creations of Phoebe Philo's designs from light-as-a-feather dresses to chunky jackets.

POMPIDOU,
BEAUBOURG
& MARAIS

# introduction

A rich mixture of old and new collide in this area of Paris. The Beaubourg, between Les Halles and the Marais, is now best known for the outrageous Pompidou Centre. Literally translated as 'beautiful market town', the Beaubourg was once a small rural community, but was enclosed within the city walls in the 13th century. West of here is the *quartier* of Les Halles, where markets were held from the early 12th century until 1969 when Victor Baltard's ten huge pavilions were demolished. Its redevelopment included large gardens and the Forum des Halles. The Marais (marshland), to the east, is one of the most interesting districts of old Paris. First inhabited by the Knights Templar, it remains substantially as it was in the 17th century after receiving a royal seal of approval with the construction of Place des Vosges. It remained fashionable until the early 18th century, and many outstanding mansions built by aristocracy have survived, although they were confiscated after the Revolution and sold to craftsmen. Still animated by trade and commerce, shops and restaurants, it has become a fashionable place to live in the last few decades.

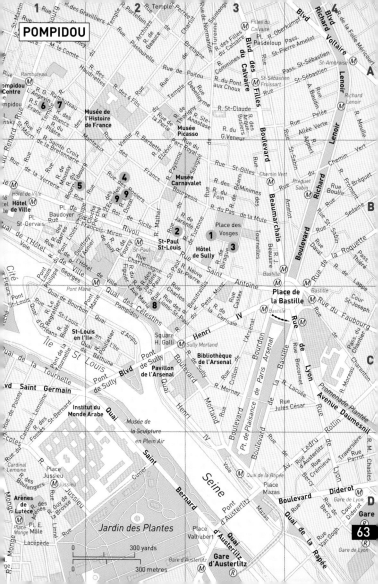

# Pompidou Centre

**Open:** Wed–Mon, 11–11; museum and exhibitions close 9pm;
Atelier Brancusi wing, 2–6 **Charges:** Entry fee except first Sun of
each month **Tel:** 01 44 78 12 33 **Web:** www.centrepompidou.fr
**Metro:** Rambuteau, Hôtel-de-Ville **Map:** p. 63, A1
**Highlights:** *Jazz* series by Henri Matisse; *Fountain* by Marcel
Duchamp; *Monochrome Blue (IKB)* series by Yves Klein; *All-black
Painting* by Pierre Soulages

The centre was named after the French president, Georges Pompidou,
who wanted to establish a centre focussed on modern creation, such
as art, theatre, music, cinema, and the spoken word. Inaugurated on
31st January 1977, it is a 15,000-ton metal box, 166m long, 60m
wide, and 42m high, with its functional elements—air-conditioning,
elevators—mainly on the exterior, in primary colours. There are seven
floors (five above ground), and one of the most daring features is the
external escalator in a glazed tube which writhes up the façade. A
novel installation south of the Centre is the fountain with amusing
coloured mobiles by Niki de Saint Phalle and Jean Tinguely.

## Modern Collections (1905–50), Level 5

**Fauvism:** This Movement was important in liberating the palette of many artists, including Georges Braque, Maurice Vlaminck and André-Derain. On no-one was the effect of the Fauve experience more emphatic than Henri Matisse. Examples of all stages of Matisse's work are here: *Algerian Woman* (1909); *Window at Collioure* (1914); *Large Red Interior* (1948; *see opposite*), which experiments with the expressive qualities of colour; several of his bronzes; and cut-outs, such as the series *Jazz* (*Tériade édition*, 1947). Matisse, in his old age, explored the technique of using brightly coloured cut-out paper shapes which allowed him to simplify his art and 'draw straight into the colour'.

**Cubism:** Its development between 1907 and 1914 is followed

**Henri Matisse:** *Large Red Interior* (1948)

through its creators, Picasso (*The Guitar Player*, 1910), and Braque (*Still Life with a Violin*, 1911) as well as the third great Cubist, Juan Gris (*Breakfast*, 1915). Robert Delaunay (*Joie de Vivre*, 1930) and his wife Sonia Delaunay (*Electrical Prisms*; 1914) were characterised by Apollinaire as Orphic Cubists for their lyrical handling of colour. Fernand Léger shifted from Orphic forms in *The Wedding* (c. 1911) to Purism in *Contraste de Formes* (1913), a rigorous, geometric form of Cubism introduced by Amédée Ozenfant and the architect Jeanneret (Le Corbusier). He later preferred monumental figures, such as *Composition with Two Parrots* (1935–49) intended to appeal to the proletariat.

**Dada:** Born in 1916 in Zurich out of the horrors of World War I, this anti-art was provocative, funny and sometimes obscene. One of its leaders, Marcel Duchamp broke through the accepted boundaries of art with his enigmatic *Nine Malic Moulds* (part of *The Bride Stripped Bare by her Bachelors, even*; 1914–5), and especially **Fountain** (1917–64). This famous 'readymade', a urinal signed 'R. Mutt', was one of the most controversial works of the era and was deliberately hidden during an exhibition of the Society of Independent Artists in 1917. The *Fountain* became the jumping-off point for future generations of artists.

**Surrealism:** This movement was developed in the 1920s, with roots in Dada, literature, Freud's theories, and the hallucinatory paintings of the Italian Giorgio di Chirico. The poetic Catalan artist, Joan Miró, was profoundly influenced by Surrealism, but shaped his own particular brand of imagery. *Blue I, II and III* (1961) is typical of the detached, floating shapes in his later work.

**Abstraction:** Dynamic abstract works by Wassily Kandinsky (*With the Black Bow*; 1912) contrast with Paul Klee's gentle *Arrow in the Garden* (1929); both were colleagues at the Bauhaus in the 1920s. Russian Constructivism, is represented by Antoine Pevsner's finely balanced geometric works and Kasimir Malevich's minimal *Black Cross* (1915), and pure abstraction was arrived at by the De Stijl group of Dutch artists, notably Piet Mondrian in *New York City I* (1942). Alexander Calder bent wire into witty sculptures including an evocation of *Josephine Baker* (1926) and went on to make delicate mobiles such as *White Disk, Black Disk* (1940–1).

**French art movements:** In the mid-20th century these included the non-geometric abstraction of Art Informel, practised by Jean Fautrier with his series *Hostage* (1945), fired by the brutality of the Second World War. The main exponent of the informal Art Brut was Jean Dubuffet, with dark, primitive, graffiti-like works such as *Dhôtel Tinted in Apricot* (1947).

**Expressionism:** The exaggerated forms and colour developed out of the symbolic use of colour by the Fauves in France, and the Brücke and Blaue Reiter groups in northern Europe. European pioneers were Frantisek Kupka (*Autour d'un Point*; 1911) and Ernst-Ludwig Kirchner (*La Toilette–Woman in Front of a Mirror*; 1913–20). Francis Bacon pays tribute to an early Expressionist in *Van Gogh in a Landscape* (1957).

## Contemporary Collections (1960–present), Level 4

**Nouveau Réalisme:** Yves Klein was the driving force behind a new perception of reality, founded in Paris in 1960, which re-interpreted the ready-mades of Marcel Duchamp (*see previous page*). Klein is best known for his monochromatic works (patented as **IKB**; International Klein Blue) which he considered deprived colour of subjective associations, usually using deep ultramarine in the belief that blue has no tangible reality. Between 1955 and 1962 he produced 194 IKBs, on canvas and as assemblage or sculpture, and scandalously used 'human brushes' to create such works as *Big Blue Anthropophagy, Homage to Tennessee Williams*

(1960). Martial Raysse's brilliant interpretations of European Pop are illustrated by *America, America* (1964), a huge neon-lighted metal hand.

**The 1960s:** In France Abstract Expressionism was headed by Pierre Soulages, the grand old man of French abstract painting who has remained constant to the possibilities of black, or black on white, and sometimes browns, on huge canvases, with designs which trace a form in space and are often reminiscent of hugely magnified Chinese characters. The works depend on paint textures and the absorption or reflection of light as, for example, **All-black Painting** (1979). Arte Povera, impoverished art, is a mainly Italian movement which appeared in 1967 to confront the materialism of the established art world by employing simple and worthless materials; the main movers were Giuseppe Penone, with *Albero* (1973), Annis Kounellis and Mario Merz. A member of a sub-group of Arte Povera, Robert Morris, produced the curiously soft but eloquent *Wall Hanging* (1969–70). Conceptual Art, the art of ideas, became a wide-ranging movement in the 1960s when Joseph Kosuth opined that art should only be conceptual and therefore must break with aesthetics, summed up in his 1968 work, *The First investigation (Art as Idea as Idea).*

**Installations and Special Works:** These include large, playful fantasies of mechanised sculpture by Tinguely, Claes Oldenburg's marginally threatening *Giant Ice Bag* (1969–70), and *Ben's Shop* (1958–73), a monumental montage of disparate objects. Niki de Saint Phalle (whose intriguing chair designs can be seen in the Musée des Arts Décoratifs; *see p. 40)* made disturbing but humorous comments on life in assemblages such as *The Bride* (1963), concerned with the role of women in society.

**1970–90:** This was a period of crisis, questioning and reaffirmation, represented in France by the Support/Surfaces group. Typical are Daniel Buren's striped installations *Jamais Deux Fois la Même* (1967–2000). Also representative is the neo-Expressionist violence of Markus Lüpertz, *Untitled MLZ 2546/00* (1992).

The small building on Piazza Beaubourg containing **Atelier Brancusi**, the reconstruction of the four studios of Constantin Brancusi, should not be missed. The studios can be viewed from different angles and include examples of his monumental sculptures, such as *Le Coq* (1935), together with plaster casts, plinths and memorabilia.

# Musée Carnavalet

**Open:** Tues–Sun 10-6, closed Mon **Charges:** Free entry **Tel:** 01 44
59 58 58 **Web:** www.carnavalet.paris.fr **Metro:** St-Paul, Chemin
Vert **Map:** p. 63, B2
**Highlights:** Apartments of the Marquise de Sévigné; *The Tennis
Court Oath* by Jacques Louis-David; *Portrait of Napoleon*

Anyone passionate about Paris will at some time want to visit the
Musée Carnavalet which illustrates the history of the city through its
fine and decorative art and occupies two of the most outstanding historical buildings in the Marais, the Hôtel Carnavalet and the Hôtel le
Peletier de St-Fargeau. Opened as a museum in 1880, the vast collection records medieval Paris, cityscapes and monuments, people and
momentous events. Some 155 rooms and objects are displayed from
Prehistoric times to the early
20th century.

**The historic Hôtel Carnavalet**

**[A] Prehistoric Paris:** The 17th-
century Orangerie (a rare survival
from the original Hôtel le
Peletier) houses Prehistoric artefacts, including two ancient dug-
out canoes (c. 2000–4000 BC),
discovered in 1991 in the Bercy
area of the city.

**[B] Sixteenth-century Paris:** Two
regal portraits from the School
of Clouet are hung here: *Mary
Stuart* (1561), the future Queen
of Scots, and *Catherine de
Medici*, widow of Henri II and
central to the religious tensions
which resulted in the St
Bartholomew's Day Massacre of
1572.

a/s/e Paris

# Musée Carnavalet

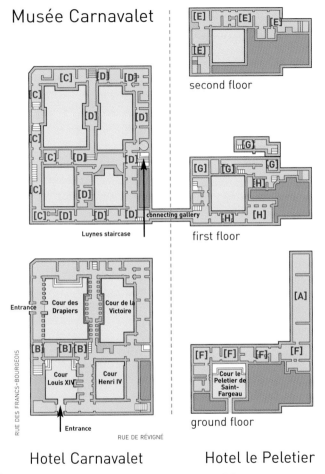

second floor

Luynes staircase

connecting gallery

first floor

Entrance

Cour des Drapiers

Cour de la Victoire

Cour Louis XIV

Cour Henri IV

Cour le Peletier de Saint-Fargeau

RUE DES FRANCS-BOURGEOIS

Entrance

RUE DE RÉVIGNÉ

ground floor

## Hotel Carnavalet

## Hotel le Peletier

[A] Prehistoric
[B] Sixteenth century
[C] Seventeenth century

[D] Eighteenth century
[E] French Revolution

[F] Early nineteenth century
[G] Late nineteenth century
[H] Early twentieth century

**[C] Seventeenth-century Paris:**
The transformation of Paris during the reigns of Louis XIII and Louis XIV is illustrated through decorative schemes inspired by Italy and interiors of grand town houses. The most remarkable early example of painted and gilded *boiseries*, wood panelling, (c. 1656) are two rooms from the Hôtel de la Rivière. Painted by Charles Le Brun, the project was one of his first major decorative commissions. The **apartments of the Marquise de Sévigné** occupied two wings of the *étage noble* of Carnavalet, from 1677 until her death in 1695 (Rooms 21–23). Her *Lettres de la Marquise*, which span 30 years, are a brilliant testament of contemporary society written in an unusually informal style for the time. The rooms contain her portrait (1662) by Claude Lefebvre, the engraving of which was used in the second edition of her *Lettres*.

**[D] Eighteenth-century Paris:**
This period encompasses the reigns of Louis XIV, Louis XV and Louis XVI. The stairwell from the Hôtel de Luynes, with trompe l'oeil paintings by P.A. Brunetti (1748), has been reconstructed, as has a rare survival of Claude-Nicolas Ledoux's decorative work in the officers'

room of the Café Militaire (1762). This was his first commission in Paris and he went on to design over 50 of the toll gates for the Farmers General city wall. During the Regency period, Rococo decoration became fashionable. The superb painted decoration from a house in Rue de la Pelleterie (Room 58) was the work of François Boucher and Jean Honoré Fragonard c. 1765.

**[E] French Revolution:** These rooms vividly retrace this turbulent period in Parisian history. Paintings and engravings recording key moments include *The Tennis Court Oath* (1789), painted by Jacques-Louis David. The painting depicts the moment when key Third Estate members (commoners who were generally outvoted at General Estate meetings) gathered in the Jeu du Paume at Versaille and swore to remain united until France had a working constitution. The huge *Fête de la Fédération* shows the Champs de Mars on 14th July 1790 when the oath to the Republic was sworn. A major part of the revolutionary history is curiosities such as a chest that carried letters from the Bastille, the keys of the Bastille, and a model of the prison cut from one of its stones. Immortalised on canvas or in sculpture are the movers and shakers of the time, such as the great orator 'beau' Barnave, the Jacobin Marat, and Robespierre, the chief architect of the Reign of Terror.

**[F] Early Nineteenth-century Paris:** This period is evoked by paintings and furnishing from the Consulate and First Empire. Here are a *Portrait of Napoleon* (1809), in the uniform of Colonel des Chasseurs de la Garde, his preferred *Nécessaire de Campagne* with 110 pieces, and his *Death-mask*. A fine portrait, *Mme Récamier Seated* (1805) by Baron Gérard depicts the famous beauty of post-Revolutionary Paris, Juliette Récamier. Rooms are also dedicated to events surrounding the Revolution of 1830 and the July Monarchy including paintings commemorating *The Erection of the Obelisk of Luxor in Place de la Concorde* (see p. 47). In the world of art and letters this was the height of the Romantic Movement, embraced by the historian Michelet, Victor Hugo, Rousseau and Mme de Stael.

**[G] Late Nineteenth-century Paris:** This section traces the story of the city during the Second Empire (1852–70),

through to 1900. Among notable objects is the Prince Imperial's grand ceremonial cradle (1856), a gift from the city to Emperor Napolèon III and Empress Eugénie on the birth of Eugène-Louis-Joseph. References to Haussmann's urban regeneration schemes include *Building of Avenue de l'Opéra* by Giuseppe de Nittis; part of the scheme which saw the city double in size with the creation of the present-day 20 *arrondissements*. The sketch *Gambetta Leaving Paris by Balloon* by Puvis de Chavannes refers to episodes during the Siege of Paris at the time of the Franco-Prussian war (1870–71), leading to the collapse of the Second Empire.

**[H] Early Twentieth-century Paris:** The museum contains two remarkable Art Nouveau interiors. The first is a private room from the Café de Paris (1899), a famous restaurant which was demolished in 1954, designed by Henri Sauvage. The second is Georges Fouquet's jewellery shop (1900) in Rue Royale, entirely created by Alphonse Mucha. Three alcoves contain personal mementos from the homes of writers Marcel Proust, Anna de Noailles and Paul Léataud.

a/s/e Paris

# Musée Picasso

**Open:** Wed–Sun, Apr–Sept, 9.30–6, Oct–March 9.30–5.30, closed 1
May, 25 Dec **Charges:** Entry fee **Tel:** 01 42 71 25 21 **Metro:** St-Paul
**Map:** p. 63, A2
**Highlights:** *Self-portrait (Autumn 1906)*; *Women Running along a
Beach*; and *Bull's Head*

The elegant 17th-century Hôtel Salé is the largest house in the Marais
and was named after the huge profits its owner made from salt tax.
The collection of works by the Spanish artist Pablo Picasso, who
spent much of his life in Paris, was acquired by the State in lieu of
death duties. The combination of modern art in a fine house is wonderful. The large collection of drawings and prints is displayed in
approximate chronological order to show Picasso's artistic development from 1894–1972.

Blue Period works, painted just after Picasso's first visit to Paris,
include a haunting *Self-portrait* (1901) at age 20 depicting the painter
in a heavy overcoat with an unshaven face, whereas the *Self-Portrait
(Autumn 1906)* shows Picasso's change of direction after discovering
Iberian art and its simplification of form. Representative of the Cubist
era (1907–15) are his first collage *Still-life with Chair Caning* (1912),
using rope and oil-cloth printed with a design of chair caning, and the
witty construction of 1915, *Violin*. His return to figurative painting
includes *Portrait of Olga Khoklova* (1917), the Russian dancer whom
he first met on a trip to Rome with Jean Cocteau, and later married in
1918. *Bathers* (Biarritz, 1918) recalls summer by the sea. The post-war
Classical Period in which Picasso dwelled on classical themes such as
bathers, and a deep analysis of three-dimensional form, is represented
by *Women Running along a Beach* (1922; *see illustration on the following
page*). The influence of Surrealism and the impact of his personal
problems at the time emerge in the aggressive *The Kiss* (1925), *Large
Nude in a Red Armchair* (1929), and *Figures by the Sea* (1931).

The mystery and sacrifice of the bull fight and the Minotaur recur
throughout Picasso's art, and is introduced in a scene of the

***Women Running along a Beach***, by Picasso, painted during his Classical Period

*Crucifixion* (1930). Towards the end of the decade, his new lover is captured in *Portrait of Dora Maar* (1937); and in 1938, he painted his small daughter, *Maya and her Doll*.

During the war period, Picasso assembled and sculpted the cryptic **Bull's Head** (1943), from bicycle parts. In this way he was one of the first artists to juxtapose unrelated objects to form something new, a technique which came out of Dada and Surrealism. *Woman with a Pushchair* (1950) is a reference to the birth of his two children with Françoise Gilot, Claude in 1947 and Paloma in 1949. The south of France inspired *Skull, Sea Urchins and Lamp on a Table* (1946) and a passionate interest in decorating ceramics is represented by a terra-cotta Spanish dish decorated with a *Bull's Eye* (1957). Animals and birds always played an important role in his work, as in *Nanny-Goat* (1951) and later works include *Déjeuner sur L'Herbe* (1960), a burlesque tribute to Manet. There are also important works collected by Picasso in the museum by Degas, Cézanne and Henri Rousseau.

# in the area

**Hôtel de Sully** (*garden open 9–7, info centre 9–6, Tues–Sat; bookshop 10–7, Tues–Sun, free entry, Tel: 01 44 61 20 00, Metro: St Paul*). The most attractive *hôtel particulier*, private mansion, in the Marais. It was probably built 1624–30 by Jean du Cerceau, the youngest in a family of Mannerist architects, and was acquired in 1634 by Maximilien de Béthune, Duc de Sully, Henri IV's minister. The courtyard, a magnificent example of Louis-XIII style, abounds in carved decorations, including six bas-reliefs in niches: the females represent the *Elements* and the males *Autumn* and *Winter*; *Spring* and *Summer* are on the garden façade. The building is now occupied by the Caisse Nationale des Monuments Historiques et des Sites, which provides information about guided tours in Paris, and by an excellent bookshop. **Map p. 63, B3**

**One of the statues at Hôtel de Sully, an elegant *hôtel particulier* in Paris**

**Hôtel de Ville** (*occasional visits and exhibitions, free entry, Tel: 01 42 76 43 43, Metro: Hôtel de Ville*). The City Hall stands on the large Place de l'Hôtel de Ville, which has been witness to important events through the centuries. Here, on 17th July 1789, Louis XVI received the newly-devised *tricolore* cockade from the Mayor. On 10th August 1792, the 172 elected commissaries gave the signal for a general insurrection. By 1805 this was the seat of the Préfet de la Seine and his council, but it had to be defended during the 1830 July Revolution. The Third Republic was proclaimed here on 4th September 1870 and, in the following March, the uprising working classes occupied the city and declared a Commune. On 24th May 1871 the Hôtel de Ville was set ablaze by its defenders and was rebuilt in 1874–84. In 1944, the Resistance movement repelled German counterattacks for five days. Nowadays, the square holds sporting activities and exhibitions, and is the beach games extension to Paris Plage, the 3km stretch of 'beach' set up in the summer between Quai des Tuileries and Quai Henri IV. **Map p. 63, B1**

**The July Column which stands in Place de la Bastille and commemorates victims of the *Trois Glorieuses* fighting of 1830**

**Place de la Bastille** (*Metro: Bastille*). Despite being one of the most famous junctions in Paris, there is no visible sign of its Revolutionary history except for a line of paving-stones in Boulevard Henri IV marking the ground plan of the famous fortress-prison. Originally a fortress, by the 17th century it had become almost exclusively a prison for political offenders, among whom were the mysterious Man in the Iron Mask (1698–1703) and Voltaire (twice). The arbitrary arrest by *lettre de cachet*, imprisonment without trial, made the Bastille a popular synonym for oppression, and among those imprisoned was the notorious Marquis de Sade, who wrote his racy novels here. On 14th July 1789, after a Revolutionary mob attacked the prison and murdered its governor, it was immediately demolished. In the centre of the Place stands the July Column erected in 1840–41 to commemorate the victims of the *Trois Glorieuses* street riots in 1830, who are buried in vaults beneath its base. **Map p. 63, C4**

**Place des Vosges** (*Metro: Chemin Vert, Bastille*). At the heart of the Marais, the Place des Vosges has a specific charm unlike any other square of Paris. Built 1606–11, the large quadrangle is surrounded by 39 houses. The king's pavilion is above the gateway in the centre of the south side, and the queen's is the corresponding building on the north (no. 28). It occupies the site of the royal Palais des Tournelles, residence of the Duke of Bedford, English regent of France in 1422 after the death of Henry V of England. It was near here that, during a tournament, Henri II was wounded during the last joust, to die ten days later. During the late-17th century, this was one of the most fashionable addresses in Paris. At number 6 is the Maison Victor Hugo (*open Tues–Sun, 10–6, closed Mon, Tel: 01 42 72 10 16*), in which the writer lived 1832–48. Authors Théophile Gautier and Alphonse Daudet, both lived at no. 8, and no. 21 was the mansion of Cardinal Richelieu. **Map p. 63, B3**

**St-Paul-St-Louis** (*open 8–8, free entry, Metro: St-Paul*). This church is a typical example of French Jesuit architecture, with a handsome Baroque entrance. It was built for the Jesuit Society by Louis XIII in 1627–41. The interior is imposing, with a 55m-high dome over the crossing. In the pendentives are medallions of the four Evangelists, and in the drum are 19th-century paintings of *Kings Clovis*, *Charlemagne*, *Robert le Pieux* and *St-Louis*. The church retains the original clear glass with floral friezes and is particularly well endowed with paintings, including *Christ in the Garden* (1827) by Delacroix, *St Louis Receiving the Crown of Thorns* (1639), and *Louis XIII offering a Model of the Church to St Louis* by Simon Vouet. **Map p. 63, B2**

# eat

**①** **€€€ L'Ambroisie**, *9 Place des Vosges, Tel: 01 42 78 51 45, open Tues–Sat, noon–1.45, 8–9.45; closed part of Feb and Aug, Metro: Bastille, St-Paul.* For a major blow-out and damn the expense, this famous and wonderful restaurant occupies the exquisite interior of the 17th-century Hôtel de Lynes. The Ambroisie lives up to its three-Michelin-star reputation and chef Bernard Pacaud tunes his perfectly cooked dishes to the seasons using foie gras or partridge, seafood or chestnuts, truffles or fresh herbs. Tastes and textures are sophisticated: among his specialities are *feuillantine de langoustines aux graines de sésame, sauce au curry; suprême de pigeon de Bresse au jus tranché,* and *tarte fine sablée au chocolat, glace à la vanilla.* The quality of the restaurant guarantees a high ratio of lackeys to customers. **Map p. 63, B3**

**②** **€€€ L'Osteria**, *10 Rue de Sévigné, Tel: 01 42 71 37 08, open Mon 8–10.30, Tues–Fri noon–12.30, 8–10.30, closed Aug, Metro: St-Paul.* An Italian restaurant whose reputation for risotto is unequalled, but is so discreet that there isn't a sign or menu to advertise it. It is all simplicity inside, small and very busy, but the cooking is marvellous and sought after by glitterati. Toni also prepares tasty gnocchi with white truffles, and spaghetti and tiramisu are all delicious. **Map p. 63, B2**

**③** **€€ Coconnas**, *2 Place des Vosges, Tel: 01 42 78 58 16, open Tues–Sun, noon–2.15, 7.30–10.15. Metro: Chemin-Vert, St-Paul.* Coconnas has had its ups and downs, but Aymeric Kräml from Brittany seems to be pulling up standards to go with the setting, and introducing some Breton touches like buckwheat *galettes* combined with elaborate fish dishes. There is, of course, the now-ubiquitous foie gras. The dining room is quite lovely with black and white tiles and red drapes, and there is also summer seating under the arches of Place des Vosges. **Map p. 63, B3**

**④** **€ L'As du Fallafel**, *34 Rue des Rosiers, Tel: 01 48 87 63 60, open Mon–Thur and Sun, 11–midnight, Fri 11–4pm, closed Sat. Metro: St-Paul.* In a street which is full of good choices to eat, here you can find quite the best falafels to take away or eat inside, especially the hummus and aubergine combination. Other dishes on offer include *merguez*, chicken curry, doner kebab and lamb schwarma. **Map p. 63, B2**

**5 € Mariage Frères**, *30–32 Rue du Bourg-Tibourg, open daily 12–7, Tel: 01 42 72 28 11, Metro: Hôtel-de-Ville.* This is a fashionable tea-room, but started out in 1854 as a tea importer and was a wholesale outlet until the 1980s. The wonderfully old-fashioned, aromatic shop has 450 teas to choose from as well as tea-making accessories. The tea-room, which is incredibly popular, also serves brunch and light lunches. They know, of course, how to make an excellent pot of tea to accompany a luscious French pastry. **Map p. 63, B1**

**6 € Pain, Vin, Fromages**, *3 Rue Geoffroy l'Angevin, Tel: 01 42 74 07 52, open daily 7pm–11.30pm, closed Aug, Metro: Rambuteau.* Tucked away behind the Pompidou are all kinds of cheesy delights. It's quite pricey, but you make your own selection of cheese platter. There are hot cheese dishes on offer as well, such as fondues, *racklettes*, *tartiflettes* and *vacherin*, specialities of the Haute-Savoie region in eastern France. Excellent bread and wine are a perfect balance to the cheeses. **Map p. 63, A1**

**7 € Le Potager du Marais**, *22 Rue Rambuteau, Tel: 01 42 74 24 66, open daily noon–midnight. Metro: Rambuteau.* This miniscule veggie and 'bio' restaurant seats just 28 at long tables along each side of the narrow space. It is extremely popular, so book if possible. The atmosphere is friendly and the food is fresh, with a fair number of choices including *sautés de légumes au tofu, de la fondue de poireaux grantinée au comté*, and *tartelettes au chocolat pimente*. **Map p. 63, A1**

**8 € Le Rouge Gorge**, *8 Rue St-Paul, Tel: 01 48 04 75 89, open Mon–Sat 12–3 & 7.30–11, closed Mon and Aug, Metro: St-Paul.* This charming wine bar (small *cave* downstairs) and restaurant has a limited menu and even more limited space. It has no pretensions, and is very relaxed and is the sort of charming café that you always hope you'll run across, which feels 'authentic'. Cooking is on the spot and the helpings are generous (enormous *assiette de crudités*). Excellent wine can be sampled by the glass. **Map p. 63, C2**

**9 € Finkelsztajn** (*two branches: Florence, 24 Rue des Ecouffes, open Thurs–Mon 10–7, Tel: 01 48 87 92 85, Metro: Hôtel de Ville; Sacha at Boutique Jaune, 27 Rue des Rosiers, open Wed–Sun 10–7, closed mid-July to mid-Aug, Tel: 01 42 72 78 91, Metro: St-Paul*), Rue des Rosiers, at the heart of the old Jewish quarter, is usually teeming and a wonderful area for food. The two Finkelsztajn delis (Florence has 1930s mosaics on the façade) combine *patisserie*, *boulangerie* and *traiteur* selling Yiddish and Eastern European specialities (eat in or takeaway) such as *vatrouchka* (cheese cake), *strudels*, and *pavés* (pastry filled with poppy seeds). **Map p. 63, B2**

# shop

Both the Beaubourg and the Marais are fun and varied places to shop, where ethnic rubs shoulders with designer, and the prices are equally diverse. The Marais is a hugely popular area for the young, airly, gay, and smart eccentrics or 'bobos' (bohemian-bourgeois) and is one of the few areas where some shops are open on a Sunday. To experience everything from kosher delis to funky designer originals, head for Rue des Francs Bourgeois (**map p. 63, B2**) and the parallel Rue des Rosiers, whereas Rue de Turenne (**map p. 63, B3**) is the place to find men's clothes and accessories. Off Rue St-Paul (**map p. 63, C2–B2**) is a labyrinth of small courtyards, Village St-Paul (*open Thur-Mon 11-7*), with antique, bric-a-brac and craft shops.

**Antik Batik**, *18 Rue de Turenne, Tel: 01 44 78 02 00, Metro: Bastille*. This is the main store of the versatile, upmarket, ethnic or 'rich hippie' designs created in France in 1992, for men, women and children. The clothes are inspired by Africa, India and the American southwest and will travel equally well to Jaipur or to Florida and wild colours, silk, beading and embroidery are used for the more exotic caftans or kurtas. Antik Batik sells clothes and accessories for all seasons, including fringed shawls, scarves and mittens, as well as very popular handbags and crocheted bikinis. **Map p. 63, B3**

**Azzedien Alaia**, *7 Rue de Moussy, Tel: 01 42 72 19 19, Metro: St-Paul*. Impeccable, sexy designs by this Tunisian-born designer can be discovered in the lofty Julien Schnabel-designed interior of his mansion-boutique. Except for Saturday (10–12.30 and 1.30–7.30) you have to ring the bell for admittance, or make an appointment. Alaia is recognised as a sculptor of form that will transform any woman. Discounted collections can be found nearby at 81 Rue de la Verrerie. **Map p. 63, B1**

**BHV**, *52 Rue de Rivoli, Tel: 01 42 74 90 00, Metro: Hôtel de Ville*. This department store is not terribly glamorous but is extremely popular as it sells everything from haberdashery to a good range of men's classic casuals at reasonable prices. In the basement is the surprisingly popular Bricolo Café. **Map p. 63, B1**

**Celis**, *72 Rue Vieille du Temple, corner Rue Barbette, Tel: 01 48 87 52 73, M: St-Paul.* This boutique specialises in hand knits. It is crammed with items mainly aimed at children. Adorable sweaters, in washable alpaca, are works of art, sprinkled with stars or abstract motifs, or more elaborate scenes including animals or mountains. There is also a huge range of knitted finger puppets, and it stocks some hand-knits for adults. **Map p. 63, A2**

**CSAO Boutique**, *9 Rue Elzévir, Tel: 01 44 54 55 88, Metro: St-Paul, Chemin Vert.* This is a large artists' co-op which embraces an art gallery, Galerie 3A, a boutique selling objects made in Senegal and West Africa (which helps homeless children in Dakar) and a restaurant, Le Petit Dakar (*Tel: 01 44 59 34 74*). The colourful imports include paintings on glass, using the *fixé sous-verre* technique special to Senegal, sold as decorative hangings or as plates, and household goods such as mad striped kettles and garish woven-plastic floor

**Gifts for sale in Litchi (*see following page*) a shop which celebrates all things kitsch**

mats, a variety of fabrics in deep earthy colour dyes, clothing, and models of the Eiffel Tower from recycled materials. **Map p. 63, B2**

**Issey Miyake**, *3 Place des Vosges, Tel: 01 48 87 01 86, Metro: St-Paul.* The revolutionary Japanese designer of novel and beautiful, but expensive, fashions for men and women. This is his main store, but his innovative second line, **Pleats Please** (*3bis Rue des Rosiers, Tel: 01 43 14 78 78, map p. 63, B2*) features clothes made from permanently pleated fabrics. Another of his concepts is **A-POC** (*47 Rue des Francs Bourgeois, Tel: 01 44 54 07 05, map p. 63, B2*), a 'cut-it-yourself' collection. It just takes a pair of scissors and imagination to turn a seamless tubular wool jersey into a desirable item of clothing, without any stitching. **Map p. 63, B3**

**L'Eclaireur**, *3ter Rue des Rosiers, Tel: 01 48 87 10 22, Metro: St-Paul.* This is one of the most trendy and popular shops in Paris, which has existed for around 20 years, and has offshoots in other parts of the city. Meaning 'trailblazer', it is a very enjoyable and sophisticated place to seek out innovative high-fashion accessories and clothes for women by top designers, with the assistance of particularly helpful staff. The men's store is at the end of the street, on 12 Rue Malher (*Tel: 01 44 54 22 11*). **Map p. 63, B2**

**Litchi**, *4 Rue des Ecouffes, Tel: 01 44 59 39 09, Metro: St-Paul.* A bizarre *boutique-tendance* which celebrates the kitsch in everything, including—or especially—religious objects and embraces a spirit of well-being with an Asian flavour. Cult items include icons, magic objects and pretty lucky bracelets. There are also paintings, picture frames (*see illustration on previous page*), lamps and bags, as well as a bar which serves fruit cocktails and vegetarian soups. **Map p. 63, B2**

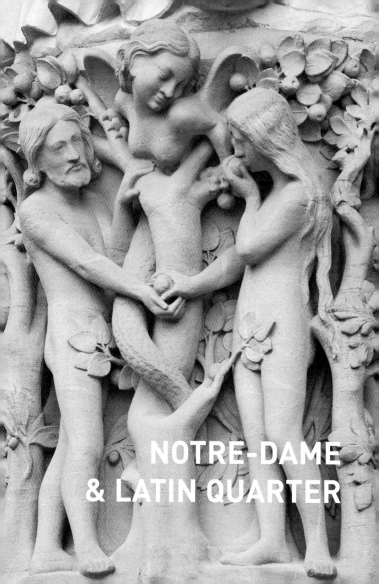

NOTRE-DAME
& LATIN QUARTER

NOTRE-DAME

# introduction

At the heart of Paris, where the River Seine widens, are two islands, the Ile de la Cité and the Ile St-Louis. Totally different in character, they each have their charms. The larger Ile de la Cité, the geographic centre of Paris and site of the original Gallic settlement of Lutèce, has a long and important history. This is reflected in its prestigious monuments such as the imposing cathedral of Notre-Dame de Paris, and Sainte Chapelle, a royal chapel. Solemn 19th-century buildings associated with law and justice occupy much of the island, but more intimate are the Marché aux Fleurs, Place Dauphine, and small public gardens. Of the seven bridges linking the island to the mainland, the 16th-century Pont Neuf, in two sections, is the oldest in Paris; and behind Notre-Dame a footbridge leads to the smaller Ile St-Louis. This discreetly elegant backwater has beautiful 17th-century façades, the immaculate little Baroque church of St-Louis-en-l'Ile, and the local Bertillon ice-cream. On the Left Bank (*Rive Gauche* or south of the river), opposite the islands is the lively Latin Quarter, whose title is a reminder of the language spoken by the medieval scholars of the University of Paris. Many centuries later it is still a student quarter, and in May 1968 was the focus of student riots. Slightly seedy in places, the old streets around Boulevard St-Michel are irresistible to visitors.

*Page 83*: **A detail from the west front of Notre-Dame showing Adam and Eve and the Serpent (1166–75; restored)**

# Notre-Dame de Paris

**Open:** Mon–Sat, 8–6.45; Sun 8–7.45; treasury open daily 9–6; visits limited during religious services **Charges:** Free entry **Tel:** 01 42 34 56 10 **Metro:** Cité **Map:** p. 84, B3
**Highlight:** Visit to towers and *Emmanuel* bell

The oldest of Paris's great emblems, the cathedral of Notre-Dame de Paris on the Ile de la Cité, is described as the ribcage of Paris, with all its associations from pre-Christian times, royal marriages, Victor Hugo's *The Hunchback of Notre-Dame* and presidential funerals. Notre-Dame was begun in 1163, replacing two earlier churches and, despite alterations, represents a text-book example of the Gothic style from the 12th to 14th century. The cathedral provided the setting for many important events, among them the coronation of Henry VI of England in 1431, aged 10, as king of France, and the marriage of François II to Mary Stuart in 1558. In 1804, Napoleon crowned himself as Emperor in Notre-Dame, witnessed by Pope Pius VII. A century later, on 26th August 1944, a thanksgiving service followed General de Gaulle's entry into liberated Paris.

### The exterior

The west front, of three distinct levels, is a masterful design of verticals and horizontals. The central Porte du Jugement, dates from c. 1220, and the *Life of the Virgin* in the tympanum is 13th century. The *Life of St Anne and the Virgin* of the Porte de St Anne (right) are mostly of 12th and 13th century. Most other statues, including the *Gallery of the Kings of Judah*, are replacements (the originals are in the Musée National du Moyen Age; *see p. 90*). The slender spire, of oak covered in lead, was rebuilt by Viollet-le-Duc in 1860, after the original was destroyed in the 18th century.

### The interior

Despite the large clerestory windows with modern glass (1964), the interior tends to be rather sombre, and is usually very busy. The daring height of the ten-bay nave confirms the prestige of the main church in Paris, and typically Gothic are the sheer elevations with shallow mouldings which emphasise the wafer-thin walls. Thirty-seven chapels surround the nave and the east end. In the barely-defined transepts are rose-windows, with the best preserved of the 13th-century glass in the north, depicting *Kings, Judges, Priests* and *Prophets* around the *Virgin*. The south, much restored in 1737, shows Christ with *Saints, Apostles*, and the *Wise and Foolish Virgins*. The west rose, depicts scenes from *Labours of the Months* and is mostly 19th century. Against the south-east pillar at the crossing stands a 14th-century image of the Virgin as *Notre-Dame de Paris*, and its pendant is *St Denis* (18th century) by Nicolas Coustou.

The choir was completely altered in 1708–25 by Louis XIV in fulfil-ment of his father's, Louis XIII, vow to place France under the protec-tion of the Virgin should he father a son. The work was carried out by Robert de Cotte. Viollet-le-Duc added an altar behind which a *Pietà* (1723) by Coustou stands on a base by Girardon which was part of the *Vow of Louis XIII*. The statue of *Louis XIII* (south) is also by Coustou and that of *Louis XIV* (north) by Coysevox (both 1715). Of the original 114 stalls, 78 remain. The bronze angels (1713) against the apse-pillars are rare survivals of the Revolutionary melting-pot. Among the tombs is the theatrical monument by Jean-Baptiste Pigalle representing the Comte d'Harcourt (d. 1769), and the restored tomb-statues of Jean Jouvenel des Ursins and his wife (d. 1431, 1451). The Treasury shelters Louis IX's supposed relic of the *Crown of Thorns*.

The **towers of Notre-Dame** (*open daily July–Aug, 9–7.30, Sat and Sun to 11pm; Apr–June and Sept, 9.30–7.30; 1 Oct–31 Mar, 10–5.30; last entry 45mins before closing; entry fee except 1st Sun of month; closed some public holidays; Tel: 01 53 10 07 00*) are a spec-tacular visit and the climb up 387 steps is worthwhile for the distant views down-river, and close-ups of Viollet-le-Duc's steeple, the suit-ably chimerical creatures he redesigned and of the medieval flying buttresses. The visit includes an exhibition about the building and the great bell, **Emmanuel**, recast in 1686 and weighing 13 tonnes made famous by Victor Hugo's *The Hunchback of Notre-Dame* (1831) in which Quasimodo was the bell-ringer.

# Sainte-Chapelle

**Open:** daily March–Oct, 9.30–6; Nov–Feb, 9–5; limited disabled access to lower level **Charges:** Entry fee, except under 17s **Tel:** 01 53 40 60 80 **Metro:** Cité **Map:** 84, A3
**Highlights:** 13th-century stained glass

The Sainte-Chapelle is a small but enthralling church, celebrated for a remarkable concentration of medieval stained glass set in a building of exceptional lightness and delicacy. Built by saintly Louis IX (he was later canonised by Pope Boniface VIII) and dedicated in 1248, it was designed as the chapel of the royal palace and the resting place for precious and costly relics acquired from the Emperor of Constantinople.

La Sainte-Chapelle consists of two superimposed chapels lined by a narrow staircase. The lower one was used by royal servants and retainers. The upper chapel was reserved for the royal family and the court. It is in the upper chapel, with its lofty windows and **medieval stained glass**, that the true beauty of the building is revealed. A virtuoso achievement of medieval architecture, the structure supports walls of richly coloured glass totalling almost 1,400m square. A large proportion of the stained glass is 13th century, skilfully restored in 1845. Each window reads from left to right and from bottom to top. In the three east windows are: on the left, scenes from the *Life of St John the Evangelist* and the *Childhood of Christ*; the central one, considered the most outstanding, dwells on *Christ's Passion*; and on the right are the *Stories of St John the Baptist* and of *Daniel*. All the other windows, bar one, have Old Testament scenes, reading from northwest: *Genesis, Exodus, Numbers, Deuteronomy* and *Joshua, Judges*, and *Isaiah* and the *Rod of Jesse*. From the southeast are *Ezekiel, Jeremiah and Tobit, Judith and Job, Esther*, and the *Book of Kings*. The southeast window, the least well preserved, depicts the *Legend of the True Cross* including scenes of the *Translation of the Relics to Paris* by St Louis. The 86 panels from the *Apocalypse* in the large, flamboyant rose-window were a gift of Charles VIII in 1485.

**The crowning glory of the Ste-Chapelle is its 13th-century stained glass**

# Musée National du Moyen Age

**Open:** Wed–Mon 9.15–5.45, closed Tues **Charges:** Entry fee, except 1st Sun of month and under-18s **Tel:** 01 53 73 78 16 **Web:** www.musee-moyenage.fr **Metro:** Cluny-la-Sorbonne **Map:** p. 84, C2 **Highlights:** Gallo-Roman baths remains; *The Lady and the Unicorn* tapestry; the *Golden Rose*

The intimate Museum of the Middle Ages is famous for its collection of tapestries. It is housed in the Hôtel de Cluny, a rare surviving example in Paris of medieval domestic architecture. The property was originally acquired by the Abbey of Cluny (Burgundy) to establish a residence in the university area and dates from c. 1490. Louis XII's widow, Mary Tudor, was among those who lived here briefly in the early 16th century. At the Revolution, the building became national property, and in 1833 was filled with the treasures collected by Alexandre du Sommerard. The collection of medieval arts and crafts is exhibited thematically in 22 small rooms over two floors.

### Ground Floor

The oldest tapestry in the museum depicts *The Resurrection* (c. 1420). Other fragile textiles and embroideries (6th–14th century), shown in rotation, include Coptic or Byzantine works. Among them is the outstanding English early 14th-century *Embroidery with Leopards*, in gold on velvet.

Small objects include intricately carved ivories (4th–12th centuries) such as the sensual *Ariadne* from Constantinople. On a larger scale are Romanesque capitals from the abbey church of St-Germain-des-Prés (*see p. 96*), original statues from Sainte-Chapelle (*see previous page*), and sculptures removed from Notre-Dame (*see p. 86*), including the original heads from the gallery of the *Kings of Judah*.

The remains of the **Gallo-Roman baths** incorporate the best-conserved vestige of Roman Paris. They were probably built during the 1st century and modified c. 212–217 AD. The *frigidarium* is unique in

**The exquisite 15th-century *The Lady and the Unicorn* tapestry, woven in silk**

France in that it still has its 2nd-century vault intact and the *piscina* has survived, but there are partial ruins of the *tepidarium*, *caldarium* and *palestra* (gymnasium).

## First Floor

A tapestry with 23 episodes of the *Life of St Stephen* was commissioned c. 1500 for Auxerre Cathedral (Burgundy). Although never restored, the colours are still strong and every painstaking detail is clearly depicted. The most famous of the museum's tapestries is, however, the series of **The Lady and the Unicorn** (*see illustration on previous page*). The six, exquisite *millefleurs* tapestries were commissioned by Jean le Viste, a Lyonnais lawyer whose family arms of a blue band with crescents on a red background are repeated in the designs. Probably designed by a Parisian artist, they were woven in silk and wool in the Netherlands in 1484–1500. The tapestries went unnoticed for a long time in a Château in the Creuse region of central France, but were brought to public notice in the 19th century by Prosper Merimée, Inspector of Historic Monuments, and the writer Georges Sand. With rich red backgrounds, blue islands of colour and different tree varieties, they are scattered with thousands of delicate flower, animal and bird motifs. In each, the Lady appears in different attire and is flanked by the mythical, elusive unicorn, symbol of purity, as well as a lion, and sometimes a monkey and pet dog. Five panels present the theme of the Senses: *Taste*, *Hearing*, *Sight*, *Smell* and *Touch*. In isolation is the sixth tapestry in the series known by the enigmatic motto embroidered on it, *A mon seul désir* (To my only desire), which shows her returning jewels to a casket held by her maid. Its iconography remains a mystery.

Also exceptional is the elegant **Golden Rose** (1330), of gold and coloured glass, given by the Avignon Pope John XXII to a Count of Neuchâtel, as a gift for his support in battle.

Among religious carvings and paintings from all parts of Europe are numerous representations of Virgins and female saints, including an early 16th-century *Virgin Reading to the Child* from the Lower Rhine and finely carved retables include the *Altarpiece of the Blessed Sacrament* (1513) from the Brabant, representing the *Mass of St-Gregory* and the *Last Supper*.

# in the area

**Arènes de Lutèce** (*open summer 9–9.30; winter 8–5.30, Metro: Jussieu*). What remains of the 1st-century Gallo-Roman amphitheatre, built for 17,000 spectators, is now used for picnics or playing *boules*. Originally used for fights as well as theatre performances, it fell into ruin in the 3rd century and was then used as a necropolis. Over the centuries much of the stone was removed and it gradually disappeared from view until 1869, when construction works uncovered part of it. Victor Hugo championed its salvation, and Dr J.-L. Capitan, after whom the garden is named, restored the ruins to their present state in 1917–18. **Map p. 84, D3**

**Institut du Monde Arabe** (*open 10-6, closed Mon, entry fee, Tel: 01 40 51 38 38, Metro: Jussieu*). This sleek and complex building of 1987 by Jean Nouvel has a total of 11 floors (nine above ground) and is arranged around an interior court or *ryad* with glass lifts and a terrace. The south

**The striking façade of the Institut du Monde Arabe, designed by Jean Nouvel**

façade's unique window shutters, or *moucharabiehs*, expand and contract in reaction to the sun's intensity. Founded to further cultural and scientific relations between France and some 21 Arab countries, there is a small museum dedicated to Arabic and Islamic art and civilisation. From the roof is a bird's-eye view of Notre-Dame, and there are two restaurants and a shop. **Map p. 84, C4**

**Jardin des Plantes** (*gardens open all year sunrise to sunset; greenhouses Wed–Mon 10–5, Sat, Sun, public hols & April–Sept 1–6; Museums Wed–Mon 10–5; Ménagerie daily 9–5.30; Grande Galerie 10–6, closed Tues & 1 May; free entry to gardens, entry fee to others, Tel: 01 40 79 30 00, Metro: Jussieu, Gare-d'Austerlitz*). The royal garden created in 1626 opened to the public in 1640, and became the Museum of Natural History in 1793. It encompasses several museums, galleries and greenhouses. The gardens have formal beds, a fanciful hillock, la Butte encased in a maze, an Alpine garden and vines. Animals kept in the gardens at Versailles were moved to the Ménagerie in 1792 and it now has over 1,000. The theme of the Grande Galerie de l'Evolution unfolds the drama of evolution in a quite magical way. **Map p. 84, D4**

**Palais de la Cité-Conciergerie** (*open daily, April–Sept 9.30–6.30, Oct–March 10–5, closed public hols, entry fee, Tel: 01 53 73 78 50, Metro: Cité*). The Conciergerie is best known as the prison where, after the Revolution, 2,780 condemned Royalists and Jacobins, including Marie-Antoinette and Robespierre, awaited execution. It started out, however, in the 13th century as a royal residence built by Philippe IV (of which the three round towers facing the river are vestiges). The visit begins with the vast 14th-century Hall of the Men-at-Arms where 2,000 people could be fed, and the smaller Guardroom. The four western bays, known as the Rue de Paris, after 'Monsieur de Paris' the Revolutionary executioner, lead to what remains of the Revolutionary Prison, mainly reconstructed, on two floors. This sad place includes Marie-Antoinette's chapel and cell, cells for the wealthy and poor, lists of the condemned, and memorabilia relating to the prisoners. **Map p. 84, A2**

**Panthéon** (*open April–Sept 10–6.30, Oct–March 10–6, entry fee, Tel: 01 44 32 18 00, Metro: Cardinal-Lemoine*). The monumental dome was built as a result of the vow taken by Louis XV in 1744 to rebuild the church of Sainte-Geneviève should he recover from an illness. The building work, begun in 1755 and directed by J.-G. Soufflot, was only completed after

**The magnificent Panthéon dome, begun in 1755**

the Revolution. In 1791, the Constituent Assembly decided it should become a shrine to France's great men and women such as Victor Hugo, Voltaire, Zola, Jean Moulin and Marie Curie. Inside is a reconstruction of Foucault's pendulum experiment of 1852, proving the rotation of the earth. The colonnade around the dome provides views of Paris (*open from April to Oct*). **Map p. 84, D3**

**St-Etienne-du-Mont** (*open Tues–Sun 8–7.30, Mon 12–7.30, closed 12–2 Sat, Sun and school holidays, free entry, Tel: 01 43 54 11 79, Metro: Cardinal-Lemoine*). This unusually pretty late-Gothic church with Renaissance decoration was built 1491–1586 on the hill where Sainte Geneviève, patron saint of Paris, was buried c. 502. It has sheltered the saint's shrine since the Merovingian abbey church was destroyed in 1802. The outstanding feature of the church is the only existing rood screen in Paris, built 1525–35 and attributed to Philibert de l'Orme. A virtuoso piece of stone carving, it has magnificent sweeping spirals at either side of the central pierced balustrade. South of the choir is the copper gilt shrine (1853) of Sainte Geneviève, containing a fragment of her tomb. There are 12 superb 17th-century windows in the charnier gallery behind the apse. **Map p. 84, D3**

**St-Germain des Prés** (*open 8–7, visits to Chapel St-Symphorian with guided tour in French Tues and Thur at 1.30, free entry, Tel: 01 55 42 81 18, Metro: St-Germain des Prés*). The church of St-Germain des Prés once stood in the meadows (*prés*). It was part of a great Benedictine Abbey founded in 558, where St Germanus, Bishop of Paris (d. 576) was interred and it became the mausoleum of the Merovingian kings. The present church was begun in the 11th century, and is the only one in Paris with considerable surviving Romanesque work. The stark St-Symphorian Chapel, just inside the door (right), is the old Merovingian necropolis. The sculpted capitals in the main body of the church are copies of the originals in the Musée National du Moyen Age (*see p. 90*), except the northwest corner. Among important tombs are those of Olivier and Louis de Castellan, by Girardon, killed in the king's service in 1644 and 1669 respectively, and Lord James Douglas (1617–45), commander of Louis XIII's Scots regiment. The next chapel contains the tombstone of the philosopher Descartes (1596–1650). **Map p. 84, B1**

**St-Sulpice** (*open 7.30–7.30, free entry, Tel: 01 42 34 59 98, Metro: St-Sulpice*). The church of St-Sulpice is a fine Italianate building of imposing size. Begun in 1646 to replace an older church, work did not halt until 1780 with the completion of the 73m high north tower—the south tower

**The organ in the church of St-Sulpice, one of the largest in existence**

remains unfinished. Highlights of the interior are the frescoes by Delacroix (south lateral chapel) representing *St-Michael Vanquishing the Devil* (vault), *Jacob Wrestling with the Angel* and *Heliodorus Chased from the Temple* on the walls. Delacroix lived nearby (on Place de Furstenberg) while he carried out this work. The spacious Baroque interior boasts one of the largest organs in existence (6,588 pipes) built in 1781. The case is by J.-F. Chalgrin, and the statues by Claude Clodion. Opposite the entrance, two huge *Tridacna giga* (giant clam) shells presented to François I by the Venetian Republic, are used as holy-water stoups. A major attraction of St-Sulpice is a meridian line in the transepts, which runs between a bronze table (south) and a marble obelisk (north). The sun, passing at noon, strikes the obelisk during the winter solstice and the bronze table during the spring and autumn solstices. **Map p. 84, B1**

# eat

Secreted in the ancient streets and squares of the islands, the Latin Quarter, Boulevard St-Michel and Boulevard St-Germain is a wide range of cafés, bars and restaurants. The Café de Flore and Les Deux Magots have always been famous as hang-outs for artists and writers, likewise Brasserie Lipp and they make great places to drop in for a coffee or a drink. Less salubrious, but also perhaps less serious or expensive, are the art-student bars around the Beaux Arts (**map p. 84, A1**).

**①** **€€€ Atelier Maître Albert**, *La Rôtisserie, 1 Rue Maître Albert, Tel: 01 56 81 30 01, open Mon–Fri 12–2.30, Sun & Wed, 6.30–11.30, Thur–Sat, 6.30–1am, Metro: Maubert-Mutualité.* This elegant and understated venue is in a small street on the Left Bank. It became part of Guy Savoy's empire in 2004, and was transformed into a fash-ionable and expensive address where traditional and modern marry successfully in the cuisine and décor. Using neutral tones, bare stone and a large fireplace, each table is in a pool of light to give diners a certain intimacy. The kitchen is open-view, with a huge *rôtisserie centrale* where the meat and fish is cooked by chefs in *toques*. Dishes are a blend of grandmother's cooking and mod-ern chic, with seasonal choices for starters, grilled fish or meat for mains, and excellent puds. **Map p. 84, B3**

**②** **€€€ Le Bélier**, ▬ *13 Rue des Beaux-Arts, Tel: 01 44 41 99 00, open Tues–Sat 12.30–2, 7.30–21.45, Metro: St-Germain-des-Prés, Rue du Bac, Mabillon.* This discreet and elegant restaurant, announced by the ram's head above the entrance to the hotel called 'L'Hôtel' (*see p. 13*), is open to non-residents from midday and in the evening. Just as discreet and elegant is the food prepared by the charming young chef, Philippe Bélissent, and the excellent and friendly service (English spoken). The tiny but plush restaurant has seating for just 40 covers, and looks out onto the patio and its fountain. At the bar you can work up an appetite with cocktails named after some of the most famous patrons of the hotel, such as Oscar Wilde and the entertainer Mistinguette. The food, which is excellent and not too quirky, is expensive but not outrageously so. **Map p. 84, A1**

**③ €€ Alcazar**, *62 Rue Mazarine, Tel: 01 53 10 19 99, open daily 12–2.30, 7–1am, Metro: Odéon.* Terence Conran's venture was considered audacious by Parisians in 1998, but the ultra-simple décor in an elegant, mirrored brasserie style, pleasant service and good quality menu, made it popular. There are wide-ranging *menus du jour* combinations at midday, as well as a dinner menu, and from Monday to Friday Fish & Chips is the *plat du jour*. The dishes are fairly traditional, well cooked and presented. The Mezzanine is a comfortable bar for cocktails or a light dinner, and music from Wednesday to Saturday with top-class DJs. **Map p. 84, B2**

**④ €€ La Bastide Odéon**, *7 Rue Corneille, Tel: 01 43 6 03 65, open Tues–Sat 12.30–2, 7.30–10.30, closed Aug, Metro: Odéon.* This is a well-patronised restaurant for its dependable bul in no way run-of-the-mill cooking, which combines ingredients and inspiration mainly from southern France, and depends in part on seasonal availability. The decor is unpretentious and comfortable, in warm colours, and the lunch *formule* changes weekly. From the à la carte selection, you might start with *sardines marinées au vinaigre de vin vieux*, *piperade de poivrons doux*, and follow on with *fin râgout de queue de bœuf Hereford*, *tranche d'aubergine et foie gras grille*. Among the good dessert selection is *moeilleux mi-cuit au chocolate valrhona, glace vanilla*. **Map p. 84, C2**

**⑤ €€ Les Bouquinistes**, *53 Quai des Grands-Augustins, Tel: 01 43 25 45 94, open Mon–Thur noon–2.30, 7–11; Fri noon–2.30, 6.30–11.30; Sat 6.30–11.30, Metro: St-Michel.* An appealing, upbeat address, owned by master chef Guy Savoy, assures professional service. It remains popular, even hectic, although it may have lost a little of its initial edge. The sleek setting on the banks of the Seine overlooks the bookstalls it is named after, and Magdala de Beaulieu Caussimon's cooking is beautifully presented. There are a number of seafood dishes, but favourites are *escargots et champignons poêles, gnocchi à l'huile de ciboulette* for starters, followed by tender faux-filet of Hereford beef, or *saumon d'Ecosse façon 'tournedos', tagliatelles fraiches et ricotta*, and honey-roasted fresh figs with blackcurrant ice cream. **Map p. 84, A2**

**⑥ €€ Brasserie Lipp**, *151 Boulevard St-Germain, Tel: 01 45 48 53 91, open daily 10–2am, Metro: St-Germain-des-Prés.* This famous rendezvous founded in 1889 remains reassuringly unchanged, with painted ceramic and mosaic panels. Drop in for a drink or traditional Alsatian brasserie fare (no reservations), and you may glimpse a politician or celebrity, although those who are known, or in the know, are elevated to the upper floor, while the ordinary tripper, unless determined, will be relegated to the ground floor. Wherever, you can still admire the frenetic activity of well-choreographed waiters, and enjoy a hearty stuffed pigs trotters, *choucroute* or *steak tartare*, and its famous *mille-feuille*. **Map p. 84, B1**

⑦ **€€ Fogón St-Julien**, *45 Quai des Grands-Augustins, Tel: 01 43 54 31 33, open Tues–Fri 7–midnight, Sat, Sun noon–2.30, 7–midnight, Metro: St-Michel*. Excellent traditional Spanish cooking with several different types of paella, as well as tapas, savoury and sweet. Altogether a good eating experience in a very sleek setting. **Map p. 84, B2**

⑧ **€€ Le Procope**, *13 Rue de l'Ancienne Comédie, Tel: 01 40 46 79 00, open Mon–Wed, noon–midnight, Thur–Sun, noon–1am, Metro: St-Michel, Odéon*. Founded in 1686 and still in business. A famous coffee shop during the Enlightenment, it was frequented by Voltaire, Rousseau and Diderot, and was arguably the birthplace of the latter's Encyclopaedia. Now considered something of a tourist trap, this wonderful building on three floors is worth visiting. The restaurant specialises in *fruits de mer*, and has an extensive menu of dishes. Among its specialities it lists *tête de veau en cocotte comme en 1686*, *le traditionel coq au vin*, and *epaule d'agneau de 7 heures*. **Map p. 84, B2**

⑨ **€€ Chez Réné**, *14 Boulevard St-Germain, Tel: 01 43 54 30 23, open Tues–Sat 12.15–2.15, 7.45–10.30,*

*Metro: Maubert-Mutualité*. This is a great example of a classic Parisian bistro, and what's more it has conserved its 1950s décor. Service is down to earth, as is the cooking, which delivers timeless favourites such as *cochonnailles* (pork), *boeuf bourgignon* and profiteroles, and the fish can also be recommended. **Map p. 84, C4**

⑩ **€€ Mon Vieil Ami**, ▪ *69 Rue St-Louis-en-l'Ile, St-Louis, Tel: 01 40 46 01 35, open noon–2.30pm, 7–10.30, Metro: Pont-Marie*. What better combination than great cooking and Ile St-Louis. A small, chic restaurant under the aegis of Antoine Westermann, three-star chef of Buerehiesel in Strasbourg, this is a minimalist and comfortable version of a bistro, with a 'communal' table down one side, and small intimate tables on the other. The excellent cooking is based on the cuisine of Alsace, with a great reputation for food and fragrant white wines. A glass of Pinot blanc d'Alsace is the *apéro*, a loaf of *pain de campagne* is sliced, and the service is admirably professional. To begin, pumpkin soup with sour cream (in season), or the *pâté en croute* (an up-market raised meat pie), *crème d'escargots*, or vegetables sautéed in butter and served in a vegetable stock. For mains braised pork, or sweetbreads with noodles and wild mushrooms, crispy *filet de lieu* (white fish) with celeriac mousse and leeks, and caramelised *choucroute*. The *tarte au chocolat* is always a favourite. The price of the set menu including three courses is remarkably reasonable, as is the wine. **Map p. 84, B4**

**11** **€€ Rhubarb**, *18 Rue Laplace, Tel: 01 43 25 35 03, open daily Sept–June 5pm–2am, July–Aug 7pm–2am, Metro: Maubert-Mutualité*. Close to the Panthéon, Rhubarb is a funky, scruffy bar with a couple of rooms including a cellar. It attracts an international student clientele of anglophones, and serves excellent cocktails including Martinis (happy hour up to 10pm), which are inexpensive as well as generous. **Map p. 84, C3**

**12** **€€ Yen**, *22 Rue St-Benoit, Tel: 01 45 44 11 18, open Mon–Sat noon–2, 7.30–10.30, Metro: St-Germain-des-Prés*. High standard and beautifully delicate Japanese cooking is served here in trendy, minimalist surroundings on two floors. Specialities include excellent *tempura* and buckwheat noodles, *soba* and *inaka*, and dishes such as *mijoté de porc à la japonaise avec pamplemousse et épinard*, and *salade de thon cru et d'avocat avec sauce de soja et wasabi*. The deluxe lunch consists of bite-sized samples served in a bento box. **Map p. 84, B1**

**13** **€€ Ze Kitchen Galerie**, *4 Rue des Grands-Augustins, Tel: 01 44 32 00 32, open Mon–Fri 12–2.30, 7–11, closed Sat lunch and Sun, Metro: St-Michel*. It is clear that chef William Ledeuil, who has travelled to Southeast Asia, was bowled over by the fragrances and ingredients of Thailand, Vietnam and Japan, which infuse his cooking. Favourites to choose from include *Ledeuil's bouillons*, such as shrimp thai broth, and sweet potato aïoli and ginger, followed by main courses (meat and fish) *à la plancha*, and heavenly desserts such as ginger and citrus fruit cake. He describes his establishment as a workshop-restaurant-gallery where he can play, invent and create, and the creations of others are exhibited on the walls. The lunch formulas are worth coming for. **Map p. 84, B2**

**14** **€ l'AOC**, *14 Rue des Fossés-St-Bernard, Tel: 01 43 54 22 52; open Mon–Sat 12–2, 7.30–11, closed Sun & Mon, Metro: Jussieu, Cardinal-Lemoine, Maubert-Mutualité*. Jean-Philippe and Sophie Lattron pride themselves on their fragrant home cooking. The top-quality produce, AOC being Appellation d'Origine Controllée, is mainly from southwest France. Starters include Serrano ham, *charcuterie* from the Aubrac and sardines from Brittany. A nice touch is that they use a rôtisserie for several dishes, and there is also *confit de canard* from the southwest and *côte de boeuf* from Normandy, ending with Toulouse ice cream. **Map p. 84, C4**

**15** **€ Au Bouillon Racine**, *3 Rue Racine, Tel: 01 44 32 15 60, open Mon–Sat 12–11, Metro: Cluny-la Sorbonne*. Installed over two floors in a splendid, restored Art Nouveau

**Coffee is served both inside and outside the historic Les Deux Magots**

building is this Belgian brasserie. Downstairs is the bar with a range of Belgian beers, upstairs is smarter. The cuisine is modern Flemish and the changing set menus are fairly easy on the wallet. **Map p. 84, C2**

**16 € Le Bar du Marché**, *75 Rue de Seine, Tel: 01 43 26 55 15, open daily 8am–2am, Metro: Mabillon*. All very *titi parisien* (i.e. a rendezvous for locals), this little bar is always packed and the street serves for the overflow on warm summer evenings. The cheery waiters wear dungarees, food is served throughout the day, and the drinks are not expensive. **Map p. 84, B2**

**17 € Brasserie de l'Ile St-Louis**, *55 Quai de Bourbon, Tel: 01 43 54 02 59, open Fri–Wed 12–1am, Thur 5–1am. Metro: Pont-Marie*. An institution, its main asset is the view across the Seine to Notre-Dame from the terrace—a great place for a beer. Inside, beyond the bar, are long rustic communal tables where basic brasserie fare is served. The location provides a good ambiance, but don't expect a gastronomic revelation. **Map p. 84, B4**

**18 € Berthillon**, *31 Rue St-Louis-en-l'Ile, Tel: 01 43 54 31 61, open Wed–Sun 10–8, Metro: Pont-Marie*. The best-known name in Parisian ice cream, and it all started here on

Ile St-Louis. It's always worth queuing to sample some of the 70 flavours of ice cream and sorbet on offer. **Map p. 84, B4**

**19** **€ Café de Flore**, *172 Boulevard St-Germain, Tel: 01 45 48 55 26, open daily 7.30–1am, Metro: St-Germain-des-Prés*. The ultimate literary café; Jean Paul Satre made the Flore his 'headquarters' and Simone de Beauvoir claimed it as a favourite amongst many cafés in St-Germain. Today, the café buzzes with the talk of young businessmen and visitors from all over the world. The interior has a certain charm to it, an inviting atmosphere that makes a visit worthwhile. The espressos are good and strong and the waiters smart in their starched white aprons and black waistcoat and trousers. **Map p. 84, B1**

**20** **€ Les Deux Magots** *Place St-Germain-des-Prés, Tel: 01 45 48 55 25, open daily 7.30–1am, Metro: St-Germain-des-Prés*. The other 'literary' café in Paris, hosting just as large a collection of arty movers and shakers from the last century: Hemingway, Scott Fitzgerald, Verlain and André Breton. Originally a drapery in the early 1800s, the name comes from a popular play at that time, The Two Magots of China, and two Chinese statues grace the main room inside. The Magots has the added advantage over nearby Café de Flore, of a large outside terrace from which to people-watch on the fascinating Place St-Germain-des-Prés. **Map p. 84, B1**

**21** **€ Guenmaï**, *6 Rue Cardinale, Tel: 01 43 26 03 24, open Mon–Sat 11.45am–3.30pm, Metro: Mabillon*. A useful address for vegetarians, this restaurant (and takeaway service) serves exclusively macrobiotic products. Open only at lunchtime, it's a friendly place with beautifully cooked crispy *tempura* and other specialities based on vegetables and pulses, with good desserts. **Map p. 84, B1**

**22** **€ Polidor**, *41 Rue Monsieur le Prince, Tel: 01 43 26 95 34, open daily noon–2.30pm, 7–midnight. Metro: Odéon*. Traditional setting with mirrors and *serveuses* '*grandes jambes*', a couple of steps from the Sorbonne. The clientele is made up half of Parisian intellectuals, half of visitors. The cooking is traditional, slow cooking, accompanied by good bread and wine. **Map p. 84, C2**

**23** **€ Le Vieux Bistro**, *14 Rue du Cloître-Notre-Dame, Tel: 01 43 54 18 95, open daily noon–2.30, 7.30–10.30, Metro: Cité, St-Michel*. Next to Notre-Dame, this old-fashioned Parisian bistro has little sophistication but is a reasonable place if you have worked up an appetite climbing the towers of the cathedral (*see p. 86*). The traditional and timeless French dishes include such classics as *poireaux vinaigrette* (leeks in vinaigrette), *cuisses de grenouille* (frogs' legs), *boeuf Bourgignon* and *tarte Tatin*. **Map p. 84, B3**

# shop

The studenty quarter of St-Michel has some fun shops, while westward, on Boulevard St-Germain and around Place St-Sulpice, the addresses get classier. Streets such as Rue Monsieur-le-Prince (**map p. 84, B2–C2**) and Rue Mouffetard (**map p. 84, D3**), in the heart of the Latin Quarter, are interesting for browsing. Rue de Buci (**map p. 84, B2**) near the crossroads of Rues Dauphine, Mazarine and Buci, is an enticing street market (closed Sun) with colourful fruit and vegetable stalls, scrumptious pastry shops and well-stocked delis.

**A.P.C.**, *3 Rue de Fleurus, Tel: 01 42 22 12 77; no. 4 (men), Tel: 01 45 49 19 15; and 45 Rue Madame (surplus), Tel: 01 45 48 43 71, Metro: St-Placide*. Close to the Luxembourg gardens, Jean Touitou's Atelier de Production et Création is the last word in well-cut cool casual togs, in understated colours. Such things as T-shirts, jeans, shoes, children's wear, and very wearable, simple women's wear are popular and moderately pricey. **Map p. 84, D1**

**Diptyque**, *34 Boulevard Saint-Germain, Tel: 01 43 26 45 27, Metro: Maubert-Mutualité*. Diptyque's line of luxury, scented candles uses only evocative natural fragrances. The 53 to chose from include *figuier* (fig leaf), *foin coupé* (freshly-cut hay), and *chevrefeuille* (honeysuckle). The candles have been marketed since 1963, and an eau de toilette, based on an old formula followed. Now, the range includes body lotions, soap, pot pourri, scented sprays which compliment the candles, and an unusual *vinaigre de toilette*. All the products are beautifully presented in well-designed packaging. **Map p. 84, C3**

**Fromagerie 31**, *64 Rue de Seine, Tel: 01 43 26 50 31, Metro: Mabillon, Odéon*. With every cheese imaginable to choose from, where do you start? A non-pasteurised Camembert, or a pungent Munster? The staff are extremely helpful and, if you can't decide, there is a cheese and wine bar and outside terrace where, you can really get to grips with the cheese challenge by opting for a tasting plate of five, seven or nine cheeses, and a glass of wine. **Map p. 84, B2**

**Games in Blue**, *24 Rue Monge, Tel: 01 43 25 96 73, Metro: Cardinal-Lemoine*. This shop has a wonderful selection of all types of board games, ancient and modern, as well as wooden jigsaw puzzles. **Map p. 84, D3**

**Kayser**, *8 & 14 Rue Monge, Tel: 01 44 07 01 42, Metro: Maubert-Mutualité*. This boulangerie/patisserie produces the sort of bread and cakes that you dream about when you're not there. No. 14 specialises in organic bread. **Map p. 84, D3**

**La Maison des Trois Thés**, *33 Rue Gracieuse, Tel: 01 43 36 93 84, Metro: Place Monge*. This is no cosy teashop in the received style but a revered address where tea-making rituals are elevated to the highest art. Demonstrations are held and tea connoisseurs can taste and purchase the very best of rare Oolong teas. The serene setting is the province of Yu Hui Tseng, the only woman among 10 Chinese tea masters in the world. She personally selects the teas during trips to Taiwan and China, and there may be as many as 1,000 to chose from. **Map p. 84, D3**

**Liwan**, *8 Rue Saint-Sulpice, Tel: 01 43 26 07 40, Metro: Odéon*. Lina Audi's boutique is a veritable Aladdin's cave of varied and breathtakingly exotic clothes, accessories and luxury household objects inspired by Africa and the Middle East. Everything is handmade, whether satin cushions, Moroccan slippers of every hue, or copper bowls. There are djellabas, jackets and caftans in heavenly colours or beautifully embroidered. It is no wonder that Liwan has a star-studded clientele. **Map p. 84, B1**

**Paris's long-established anglophone literary institution, Shakespeare and Co.**

### Bouquinistes

Unique to Paris are the open-air booksellers or *bouquinistes*, situated on both sides of the Seine, from the Quai de la Tournelle to the Quai Malaquais on the Left Bank (**map p. 84, C4–A1**), and from the Pont Marie to Quai du Louvre on the Right (**map p. 84, B4–A2**). These traditional riverside salesmen are a throwback to the time when most trading took place on the streets, and the first *bouquiniste* was recorded in 1891 on Quai Voltaire. All year round, but preferably in fine weather, the 250 or so green boxes of identical shape and size (8.2m) are opened up to display antique and uncut books, old postcards, posters and engravings. There are still occasional back copies of Paris Match and dusty old newspapers, but garish modern souvenirs have started to make an appearance. Trade never appears to be particularly brisk, but for the passer-by the stalls are a constant source of fascination.

**Pierre Hermé**, *72 Rue Bonaparte & 185 Rue de Vaugirard, Tel: 01 43 54 47 77, Metro: St-Sulpice*. The pastry and chocolate shop created by the doyen of chocolate, Pierre Hermé, is considered '*pâtisserie fashion*' by Parisians. Like the best fashion designers, he has new collections twice a year. Locals and tourists flock to his door to revel in his chocolate, which lingers on the palette like fine wine. Also on sale in his pretty and innovative shops are macaroons, chocolate drinks, *pâtes de fruit*, jams and cookbooks by Hermé. **Map p. 84, C1**

**Shakespeare and Co.**, *37 Rue de la Bucherie, Tel: 01 43 6 95 50, Metro: St-Michel*. The reputation of this secondhand bookshop (*see illustration on previous page*), and self-proclaimed institution, is perpetuated by would-be writers who staff the three floors. It was opened here by the bibliophile George Whitman (grandson of Walt) in 1951 and since then has been a centre for creativity and the arts, with regular readings by both published and unpublished writers. The original shop, on Rue de l'Odéon was established by Sylvia Beach during the inter-war years. Its fame rests on publishing James Joyce's Ulysses in 1922 and it became a popular rendezvous of inter-war American writers. **Map p. 84, B3**

EIFFEL TOWER &
MUSEE D'ORSAY

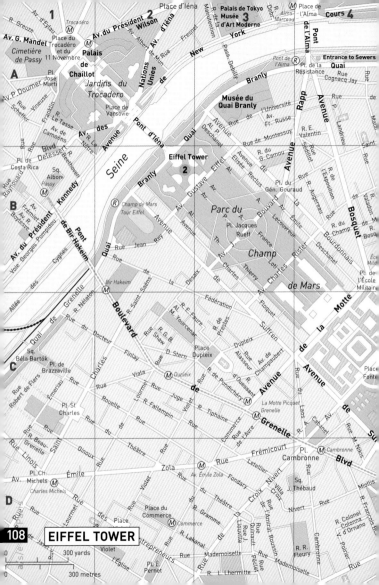

# EIFFEL TOWER

0    300 yards

0    300 metres

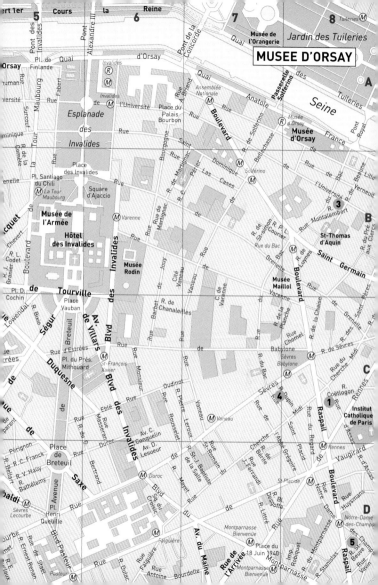

# introduction

Enduringly elegant, Faubourg St-Germain was open countryside until the Hotel des Invalides was constructed in 1670 on the western outskirts of the Abbey of St-Germain-des Prés. With the advent of the Pont Royal spanning the Seine in 1689, providing easy access to the court at Palais des Tuileries, this became the new aristocratic quarter. Many of the elegant *hôtels particuliers* built in the 17th and 18th centuries still determine its character. The ultimate emblem of Paris, the Eiffel Tower, was built on the Champs de Mars in 1889 and offers a continuous vista across the Seine. Other major attractions here are Les Invalides, the Musée d'Orsay, the more intimate Rodin and Maillol museums, and the important new Musée du Quai Branly. Major museums in southwest Paris, such as the Art Moderne de la Ville de Paris on the Right Bank, are linked to the Left Bank by Pont d'Iéna and the footbridge, Passerelle Debilly.

# Eiffel Tower

**Open:** Ascent by lift daily, mid-June–end-Aug, 9–midnight, Level 3 last departure 11; Jan–mid-June & Sept–end-Dec, 9.30–11, Level 3 last departure 10.30. Ascent on foot daily to Level 2 only, mid-June–end-Aug 9–midnight; Jan–mid-June & Sept–end-Dec, 9.30–6
**Charges:** Entry fee **Tel:** 01 44 11 23 23 **Web:** www.tour-eiffel.fr
**Metro:** Bir Hakeim, Trocadero **Map:** p. 108, B2

From most parts of Paris there is a view of the familiar outline of the Eiffel Tower which stands close to the river on Quai Branly. Its looming presence is the main focus of one of the great vistas of Paris which stretches from the Ecole Militaire down the 1km-long gardens of the Champ-de-Mars and across the Seine to the Palais de Chaillot. Even now, the audacious proportions of this masterpiece of 19th-century engineering still take your breath away.

The tower opened in 1889 for the Universal Exhibition marking the 100th anniversary of the Revolution and aroused a great deal of controversy. Originally granted only 20 years of life, its new use in radio-telegraphy in 1909 saved it. Erected by Gustave Eiffel's contracting company, the 318m lattice-work tower is composed of 18,000 pieces of metal weighing over 7,000 tonnes, while its four feet are supported by masonry piers sunk 9–14m into the ground. The design was mainly due to the engineers Maurice Koechlin and Emile Nouguier and the architect Stephen Sauvestre. It is repainted every seven years in Eiffel-Tower bronze.

On the vast Level 1 there are two light-hearted, interactive presentations providing information on the history and technology of the structure and a laser system that measures the oscillations of the summit. You can glimpse the old hydraulic pump and a section of the original spiral staircase and visit the post office, for an Eiffel Tower postmark on your card. On Level 2 are glazed portholes for an unusual view directly to ground level. At the top level, apart from the breathtaking panorama of Paris, is a reconstruction of Gustave Eiffel's office. There are two restaurants on the Tower, see p. 124.

Paris

a/s/e

# Musée d'Orsay

**Open:** Tues–Sun, 9.30–6; Thur until 9.45pm; closed 1 Jan, 1 May, 25 Dec **Charges:** Entry fee except 1st Sun of month **Tel:** 01 40 49 48 00 **Web:** www.musee-orsay.fr **Metro:** Solférino **Map:** 109, A8 **Highlights:** *Le Déjeuner sur l'Herbe* by Edouard Manet; *Absinthe Drinkers* by Edgar Degas; *Bedroom at Arles* by Vincent van Gogh; *And the Gold of their Bodies* by Paul Gauguin

National collections from the 1840s to the first decade of the 20th century assembled at the Musée d'Orsay cover all aspects of the visual arts including painting, drawing, pastels, sculpture, decorative arts and photography, but visitors come mainly for its outstanding collection of Impressionist works.

The museum, which opened in 1986, is the result of a remarkable metamorphosis of the former railway station, Gare d'Orsay (1900), into a museum. The station's huge and ornate bulk, which faces the Seine, has two great clocks and still bears the names of destinations it once served, such as Orléans and Toulouse. Some 4,000 works of art are permanently on display, arranged chronologically and thematically, in around 80 galleries over three main floors. The recommended sequence of the visits starts at Level 0 (Nineteenth century), then Level 5 (Impressionism and Post-Impressionism), and lastly Level 2 (Twentieth century).

## Level 0 (Nineteenth century)

**[A] Central aisle:** In this lucid space are 19th-century sculptures, bronzes and plasters, including Jean-Baptiste Carpeaux's *Ugolino* (1862), which led to important public commissions such as the controversial *La Dance* for Opéra Garnier, and the *Four Quarters* *of the World* for the Observatoire Fountain in the Luxembourg Gardens (*see p. 50*). The large canvas by Thomas Couture, *Romans of the Decadence* (1847), was a comment on the vices of contemporary society.

**[B] Seine Gallery:** This gallery introduces the realities of life in

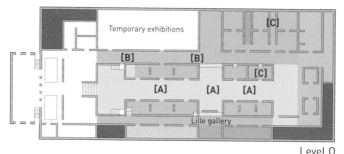

Level 0

[A] Central aisle
[B] Seine gallery
[C] Rooms 18–21

Architecture
Decorative arts
Paintings
Sculptures

the 19th century; Courbet was criticised for the blatant realism of *Burial at Ornans* (1850), shown in Room 7, because of the monumental presentation of a group of humble peasants. Further statements of developing social awareness and the dignity of honest toil are Daumier's *Washerwoman* (c. 1863), and Millet's *The Gleaners* (1857), in Rooms 4–6.

**[C] Rooms 18-21:** In contrast to the industrious, realist paintings of Daumier and Millet, landscapes painted in the open-air were pioneered by the Barbizon painters in Fontainebleau Forest, and precursors of Impressionism such as Eugène Boudin with his *Beach at Trouville* (1864).

Jongkind paved the way for Monet's swathe of red poppies, *Les Coquelicots* (1873). Edouard Manet's **Le Déjeuner sur l'Herbe** (1863; *illustrated on next page*), was considered scandalous at the time both for its subject matter and non-conformist technique. The painting, which follows in the tradition of Titian and Watteau's *fête champêtres*, or depictions of outdoor entertainment, became one of the most notorious picnics of all time. True Parisian and bourgeois revolutionary, Manet reacted against the idealism of Thomas Couture's studio and sought to reconcile style and modern life. Still provocative and inscrutable, it is now considered a masterpiece.

**Edouard Manet's *Le Déjeuner sur l'Herbe* caused a scandal when first shown**

Slightly later is *The Balcony* (1868–69), shown opposite in Room 14, a confident painting whose use of colour and dramatic contrasts proves his versatility and admiration for Goya.

### Level 5 (Impressionism and Post-Impressionism)

**[D] Rooms 29 and 30:** These collections are introduced by Fantin-Latour's *Hommage à Delacroix* of a group of painters and writers which includes Edouard Manet and Emile Zola. Degas' ***Absinthe Drinkers*** (1876) is an exercise in spatial harmony and colour but depicts addiction and despair, a theme also addressed by Zola in his book *L'Assommoir* (1877).

**[E] Rooms 31–35:** Typically hedonistic are paintings by Renoir from the 1870s to 1919 such as *Dance in the Country* (1883) and *Bal du Moulin de la Galette* (1876) in Montmartre on a Sunday afternoon, while Monet captures modern life in

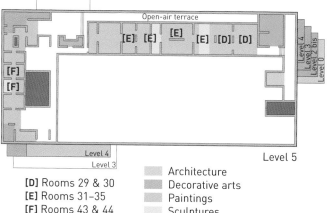

Open-air terrace

[E] [E] [E] [E] [D] [D]

[F]
[F]

Level 4
Level 3

Level 5

Level 4
Level 3
Level 2 bis
Level 0

[D] Rooms 29 & 30
[E] Rooms 31–35
[F] Rooms 43 & 44

Architecture
Decorative arts
Paintings
Sculptures

the *Gare St-Lazare* (1877) and paintings of London and Giverny in the first decade of the 20th century. Post-Impressionism contains rich pickings. There are intense and sometimes rhapsodic paintings by van Gogh including the **Bedroom at Arles** (1889).

**[F] Rooms 43 and 44:** Here are shown Gauguin's impenetrable, but richly coloured, symbolism in *La Belle Angèle* (1889) and **The Gold of their Bodies** (1901) which was painted while he lived in the South Pacific from 1875 to 1903.

## Level 2 (Twentieth century)

The splendid Salon de Thé of the old station hotel (*open for lunch and tea with a good value buffet at midday; ticket holders only, no reservations*) is a wonderful survival from the old station hotel and retains its original 1900 painted and gilded decor.

**[G] Rooms 70–72:** These rooms have paintings by the Nabis group, including works by the co-founder Maurice Denis. The

Nabis group sought to promote the teachings of Gaughin, and their name derived from the Hebrew for 'prophet'.

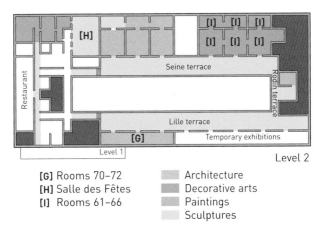

**[G]** Rooms 70–72
**[H]** Salle des Fêtes
**[I]** Rooms 61–66

Architecture
Decorative arts
Paintings
Sculptures

**[H] Salle des Fêtes:** The ballroom of the old hotel has been reinstated in all its glitzy glory with gilded mirrors and chandeliers. Alongside paintings of Belle-Epoque beauties are frivolous works by William Bouguereau, anathema to the Impressionists.

**[I] Rooms 61–66:** Among Art Nouveau and Art Deco production is jewellery by René Lalique, brilliant stained glass by Louis Comfort Tiffany and Jacques Gruba, exquisitely over-elaborated furnishings such as a chimneypiece by Hector Guimard, and the 'Nenuphars', waterlily, bedroom suite (c. 1905) by Eugene Vallin.

**Seine & Lille Terraces:** These terraces contain monumental sculpture 1780–1914, with representative works by Auguste Rodin, Camille Claudel's impressive bronze group *L'Age mur* and Emile Antoine Bourdelle, whose work is dominated by themes of conflict, power and heroism.

# Musée du Quai Branly

**Open:** Tues–Sun, 10–6.30, Thur 10–9.30 **Tel:** 01 56 61 70 00 **Web:** www.quaibranly.fr **Charges:** Entry fee except 1st Sun of month **Metro:** Alma-Marceau **Map:** 108, A3
**Highlights:** Museum building by Jean Nouvel; Mvoudi mask from equatorial Africa; textiles and costumes from Asia

The opening of the Musée du Quai Branly was the most important museum happening in Paris in 2006. The museum is devoted to non-European arts and civilisations, namely Oceania, Africa, Asia, and the Americas. Its objective is to illustrate the lifestyle of cultural and ethnic groups through some 3,500 objects. The collections are housed in an ingenious **building by Jean Nouvel**, with an eye-catching stilts design. It emerges from sloping gardens and uses deep earth-colours on the exterior, and has a 'plant wall'. Inside, a large totem pole stands in the cavernous reception area from where a ramp spirals around a glass tower containing musical instruments. The main floor is wreathed in dramatic obscurity (partly for conservation purposes), and the exhibition space flows freely between the sections. On the south side, in the Asian and Africa sectors, some 30 'boxes' contain special exhibits, and two are reserved for music. Information is widely diffused and includes interactive multimedia installations.

The objects in the collections demonstrate diversities but also similarities throughout these cultures. Common to each is the relationship between man and his gods. In the Solomon Islands this may be symbolised by a divine receptacle in the shape of a fish, or by a votive figure in Mexico of Tialoc, God of Rain and Personification of the Earth. Masks are used in a great diversity of forms and in a variety of materials, may either be animal or human, and may cover the whole head or just the face. The Hemlour masks of the Sulka people (Oceania) are rare as they were burned after the ceremony in which they were used. An anthropomorphic mask with goat's hair from Nepal represents a forest spirit, and ethnic groups of Equatorial Africa produced a huge variety of masks, some of which inspired Western artists early in the 20th century, such as the **Mvoudi mask** coloured in ochres, while the Haida people North America produced an articulated mask. The skills necessary for carving are manifold, in large or small objects, religious and secular. The range covers a Maori Hei Tiki pendant carved in jade, the pre-Dogon Androgynous figure from Mali (10th–11th century), and an anthropomorphic sculpture of a *Woman Holding her Breasts* c. 700–1100 from Costa Rica.

The backbone of the Asians collections is a very colourful array of **costumes and textiles**, representing the diversity of lifestyles, cultures and climates on the Asian continent. It illustrates the way in which raw materials, techniques of weaving and sewing, dyes and decorative elements, are applied in individual communities. Birch-tree bark is used in Siberia, elaborate jackets are embroidered from memory in Laos, and flat lengths of cloth are used in India according to Hindu ideology. The wide range of textiles and cloth from other cultures includes ancient fabrics from Pre-Hispanic Andes found in Inca tombs in Peru. The commonality in personal adornment is exemplified by a Gold crown from Southern Nias Island, Insulindia, a gold Bird Necklace with precious stones, worn by Jews in Morocco, and a silver torque from Guizhou province, China. Less costly but equally significant are Amazonian feather art and body painting, still practised today. Particular emphasis is put on recent Australian aboriginal art.

# in the area

**Les Invalides** (*open daily April–Sept 10–6, Oct–March 10–5; closed 1st Mon of month, 1 Jan, 1 May, 1 Nov, 25 Dec, entry fee, Tel: 01 44 42 37 72, www.invalides.org, Metro: Invalides*). Founded by Louis XIV for up to 6,000 wounded soldiers, this magnificent hospital, the headquarters of the Military Governor of Paris, was built in 1671–1706 by Libéral Bruant and Jules Hardouin-Mansart. The Dôme des Invalides, originally a royal chapel, has been the resting place of Napoleon's remains since 1861. His imposing tomb of red porphyry and green granite was designed by Visconti. It is placed in the crypt below the most splendid dome in France,

**The dome of Les Invalides, decorated with 12kg of gold**

which was regilded in 1989 with 12kg of gold. The buildings also contain the Musée de l'Armée, the Musée des Plans-Reliefs (models of fortified sites), the church of St-Louis, and a museum dedicated to the Ordre de la Libération and General de Gaulle. **Map p. 109, B5**

**Musée d'Art Moderne de la Ville de Paris (Palais de Tokyo)** (*open Tues–Sun, 10–5.30, Wed during temporary exhibitions, 10–10, free entry to permanent collections, Tel: 01 53 67 40 00, www.mam.paris.fr, Metro: Iéna, Alma-Marceau*). Among the collections of modern art which belong to the City of Paris at the Palais de Tokyo, all the major movements of the early 20th century are represented. There are a number of works by Robert Delaunay (*Hommage à Bleriot*; 1913–14) and Fernand Léger (*The Discs*; 1918) who celebrated the technical age. The interwar years produced Dada, Surrealism and the School of Paris as well as contrasting painters such as Jean Fautrier and Pierre Bonnard (*Nu dans le Bain*; 1936) who grappled with the problems of painting white. Post-1960s Lyrical

**Antoine Bourdelle's bronze statue, *La France*, at the Musée d'Art Moderne**

Abstractionists working in France include Hans Hartung, who owed a debt to Japanese calligraphic painting, and Simon Hantaï who worked with folded and crumpled surfaces. Two specially created large rooms conserve major decorative schemes of the 1930s: Henri Matisse's large murals, *La Danse Inachevée* (1931) and *La Danse de Paris* (1931–33), resulting from a commission from the Barnes Foundation of Philadelphia, and Raoul Dufy's mural, *La Fée Eléctricité* created for the Pavilion of Light at the 1937 Exhibition. Characteristic of the contemporary collections are *Décollages d'affiches* by Nouveau Réalists Jacques Villeglé and Raymond Hains, and Nouvelle Figuration, a 1960s revival of figurative painting practised by Valerio Adami, and Combas (*La Bataille de Waterl'eau*; 1982) in strip cartoon style. Art of 1980–2000 includes a space dedicated to works by Christian Boltanski's themes of remembrance (*Reserve du Musée des Enfants*; 1989). **Map p. 108, A3**

**Musée Maillol** (*open Wed–Mon 11–6, entry fee, Tel: 02 42 22 59 58, www.museemaillol.com, Metro: Rue du Bac*). When Aristide Maillol was 73 he found in Dina Vierny, aged 15, the ideal figure he had been modelling all his life. She later became a collector and in 1995 the Fondation Dina Vierny endowed the museum. Maillol is best known as a sculptor of monumental female nudes, such as *La Rivière* and the bronze *Pomone* (1910), although he began as a painter (*Seated Woman with Sunshade*; 1895). The museum is an interesting overview of different aspects of Maillol's creativity, including pastels, ceramics and woodcarving as well as works by Renoir, Maurice Denis and Gauguin from whom he drew inspiration. Vierny was a supporter of naïve artists, such as Louis Vivin and Camille Bombois, and of Russian non-figurative art, including works by Kandinsky and Poliakoff. **Map p. 109, B7**

**Musée Rodin** (*open Tues–Sun, April–Sept 9.30–5.45, garden to 6.45; Oct–March 9.30–4.45, garden to 5, entry fee except 1st Sun of month, Tel: 01 44 18 61 10, www.musee-rodin.fr, Metro: Varenne*). The most popular museum in Paris devoted to a single artist has works in marble, bronze and plaster, as well as memorabilia donated by Auguste Rodin to the State in 1916. It occupies the 18th-century Hôtel Biron, where the sculptor worked, and its gardens. The bronze *Gates of Hell* were inspired by Dante's *Divine Comedy* and Michelangelo's *Last Judgement* in the Sistine Chapel in Rome. Rodin described the Gates as his 'Noah's Ark' of inventions, providing him with an endless source of motifs which he re-used, in part or whole. Rodin did not carve, but modeled in plaster from which bronzes were cast. Rodin's first freestanding figure *The Age of*

Paris

a/s/e

*Bronze* (1876–77) is in the collection, as well as a bronze of the *Burghers of Calais* and many preparatory works for the monument to the writer Honoré de Balzac, the finished creation of which caused endless controversy due to Rodin's depiction of Balzac's less than Herculean physique. Rodin's assistant and lover, Camille Claudel, is also represented here. **Map p. 109, B6**

**Palais de Chaillot** (*Metro: Trocadéro*). The two wings of the Neoclassical Palais de Chaillot frame a remarkable vista towards the Eiffel Tower from a terrace flanked by gilded bronze statues. In the Trocadero Gardens which descend to the Seine are fountains with a battery of 20 water jets. The panorama encompasses the Pont d'Iéna, the Champ-de-Mars, the Ecole Militaire and Unesco, and now the Musée du Quai Branly (*see p. 117*). The Palais de Chaillot, which stands on the southeast of the Place du Trocadéro, was erected for the Paris Exhibition of 1937, replacing an earlier Palais du Trocadéro for the 1878 Exhibition. In the west wing are the Musée de la Marine (*open Wed–Mon 10–6*), and the Musée de l'Homme (*currently closed*). In the east wing is the Cité de l'Architecture et du Patrimoine (*open Mon, Wed, Fri 12–8, Thur 12–10, Sat & Sun 11–7*), a new centre of French architecture incorporating the old Musée des Monuments Français and the Institut Français d'Architecture. Beneath the terrace is the Théâtre de Chaillot, decorated by Bonnard, Dufy and Vuillard. **Map p. 108, A1**

*Spirit of the Eternal* by Rodin in the sculpture garden of his museum

# eat

In Faubourg St-Germain you won't go hungry (or thirsty). This quarter has a multitude of eating places ranging from elegant Art Nouveau to minimalist design, and from the most sophisticated and expensive to basic student bars.

**① €€€ Hélène Darroze, Restaurant and Salon**, *4 Rue d'Assas, Tel: 01 42 22 00 11, open Tues–Sat 12.30–2, 7.30–10.15, Metro: Sèvres-Babylone.* This resolutely up-market address serves beautiful food which is a modern take on the cuisine of Hélène Darroze's native southwest France. She uses the best ingredients of that region—foie gras and poultry from the Landes, beef from the Chalosse, salmon from the Adour, and milk-lamb from the pays Basque—in exquisite and imaginative dishes. Parquet floors and heavy drapes, well-spaced tables and deep tones of gold and Bordeaux, produce an all-enveloping yet uncluttered ambiance in the upstairs restaurant. Among the wonders served here are, in season, a 'truffle menu' of five courses including dessert; also typical of her creation is *foie gras frais de Landes grillé au feu de bois*, *fruits d'automne caramélisés*, *réduction de Porto* and delicious extras such as the *petits four* trolley. The Salon, downstairs (*open as above but closed Tues lunch*), has a novel approach to sampling the cooking of the master chef. From a 'tapas menu' you select four or five small but beautiful combinations among starters, mains or desserts. It's inventive, delicious, and professional. **Map p. 109, C8**

**② €€€ Jules Verne**, *2nd floor, Eiffel Tower, south pillar, Tel: 01 45 55 61 44, dedicated elevator access, open daily noon–2.30, 7–9.30, Metro: Bir-Hakeim, Trocadéro.* This is the gastronomic restaurant in the Tower. Here you reach the giddy heights in a combination of unsurpassable vistas and upmarket cuisine, which was taken over by Alain Ducasse on 1st January 2007. It gets booked months in advance. On the floor below is **€€ Altitude 95**, (*Tel: 01 45 55 20 04, open as Jules Verne*). Why not experience the hard metallic Zeppelin décor at 95m above sea level where the view is always a winner. The cooking is average and prices affordable (better value at lunchtime) compared to the Jules Verne. To be sure of a window table it is absolutely essential to book early. **Map p. 108, B2**

**③ €€ L'Atelier de Joël Robuchon**, *Rue de Montalembert, Tel: 01 42 22 56 65, open daily 11.30–3.30, 6.30–midnight, Metro: Rue du Bac*. A revolutionary venture by one of the great French chefs is this informal bistro where you sit on bar stools around an open kitchen. The influence is Spanish, the helpings are small, and the quality is superb—but a long way from haughty *haute cuisine*. No reservations are taken, just turn up from around 6.30 and be patient. **Map p. 109, B8**

**④ €€ L'Epi Dupin**, *11 Rue Dupin, Tel: 01 42 22 64 56, open Mon 7–9, Tues–Fri noon–2.30, 7–9, Metro: Sèvres-Babylone*. This small place remains incredibly popular with all Parisians because the cooking is consistently excellent and the prices reasonable, notably the set menu. François Pasteau's imaginative delights include *endive Tatin* with goats cheese, fillet of lamb with ratatouille, and citrus and chestnut *lillet chaud-froid*. The rustic bare-stone-and-beams salon is usually crammed as it seats only 50. It is essential to book. **Map p. 109, C8**

**⑤ € Le Timbre**, *3 Rue Sainte-Beuve, Tel: 01 45 49 10 40, open Tues–Sat, noon–2, 7–10.30, Mon 7–10.30, Metro: Notre-Dame des Champs*. Opened by Englishman

**Pavement dining in the chic Faubourg St-Germain**

Christopher Wright, the postage-stamp-sized bistro gets plenty of well-deserved support for its grub, whether British or other. There are unusual starters, such as beet soup laced with curry, or Jabugo ham with lentils. To follow there is *magret de canard* or sausages from the Auvergne, all served with good vegetables. **Map p. 109, D8**

**⑥ € Tokyo Eat**, *Palais de Tokyo, Site de Création Contemporaine, 13 Avenue du Président Wilson, Tel: 01 47 20 00 29, open Tues–Sun, noon–1 am, Metro: Alma Marceau, Iéna.* This half of the Palais de Tokyo has seen many metamorphoses, and when the Cinémathèque was moved out of the 1930s building, the cavernous space was not altered and became a centre of contemporary creation, with varied artworks and installations. The restaurant facing the street, is all concrete and girders, but is very fashionable and attracts a wide range of customers. This is an entertaining place to eat, with music in the evening—part of the entertainment is choosing the track (quieter at lunchtime). The cooking is imaginative and introduces a few 'eastern' touches, but is slightly unpredictable, although reasonably priced and it's certainly more fun than the café at the Museum of Modern Art in the other half of the building. **Map p. 108, A3**

# shop

In Faubourg St-Germain ultra chic and trendy designer boutiques sit alongside fashionable food stores. The likes of Armani and Sonia Rykiel have nudged their way in between the long-established retail outlets and antiquarians or staked their claim alongside legendary cafés and close to old churches. In the small streets around Carrefour de la Croix Rouge—the Rues du Cherche-Midi and du Dragon (**map p. 109, C8**)—shoe fetishists could get high on the mind-blowing number of shops selling all ranges of footwear from ultra-funky-squash-your-toes to fuddy-duddy. For yummy morsels, long-established and brand-new shops selling up-market breads, cheeses and pastries jostle for place around here, while Rue Cler (**map p. 108, B4**) promises an appetising stroll past *boulangeries* and market stalls (every morning except Monday, and some evenings) punctuated by a visit to the Café du Marché at no. 38, open from breakfast to late-night snack. The narrow, picturesque streets between the boulevard and the river have long been the exclusive domain of antiquarians, art dealers and interior designers. Le Carré Rive Gauche (www.carrerivegauche.com) is a group of around 120 antiques shops and art galleries in an area defined by Quai Voltaire and Rues du Bac, de l'Université and des Sts-Pères (**map p. 109, C8–B8**), which holds an annual event in June.

**Atsuro Tayama**, *81 Rue des Saints-Pères, Tel: 01 49 54 74 20, Metro: Sèvres-Babylone.* Softly sculpted, easy to wear clothes for women are the hallmark of Japanese designer Atsuro Tayama. He uses a limited palette—black, white, silver and red, and grey-greens in 2007—and washable fabrics which either carry bold designs from geometric to more fluid, or are plain. Tayama's deceptively simple clothes are beautifully cut and very flattering, often with a discreet sense of drama, or ruched and tucked. His range includes smart day dresses, belted trench coats, cowl-necked sweaters, soft flexible knits and leggings. **Map p. 109, C8**

**Le Bon Marché**, *22 Rue de Sèvres, Tel: 01 44 39 80 00, Metro: Sèvres-Babylone.* The sole department store on the Left Bank is very classy and the oldest in Paris. Opened by Aristide Boucicaut in 1848, the present building dates

**Antiquarian collectables for sale in Faubourg St-Germain**

from 1869–87 and the architect L.A. Boileau enlisted the help of Gustav Eiffel to build the light metal structure. Bon Marché has designer ranges, fashion accessories, menswear and kitchenware, as well as contemporary art (3rd Floor) and it holds regular exhibitions. On the 1st Floor is the Delicabar which specialises in snacks based on fruit, chocolate and vegetables. **La Grande Epicerie** (*38 Rue de Sèvres, Tel: 01 44 39 81 00*) is Bon Marché's mouth-watering gourmet food annexe, with over 200 cheese varieties, 80 types of olive oil, and where recently 15 different varieties of tomato were spotted; it also sells the ultimate in picnic goodies. **Map p. 109, C8**

**Boulangerie Poilâne**, *8 Rue du Cherche-Midi, Tel: 01 45 48 42 59, Metro: Sèvres-Babylone, St-Sulpice.* The Poilâne empire was launched here in 1932 by Pierre Poilâne, in the small neighbourhood bakery which is now run by Apollonia, his granddaughter. Among a range of delicious breads and tarts, the most famous loaves are the huge brown *miches* made with stone-ground flour and baked in a wood oven. With a strong crust and slightly sour taste, it can be bought in sections and is delicious toasted. This bread is so successful that it is sold in supermarkets all over France and exported to New York and Tokyo. **Map p. 109, C8**

**Editions de Parfums Frédéric Malle**, *37 Rue de Grenelle, Tel: 01 42 22 77 22, Metro: Rue du Bac*. Malle has created a modern and unusual boutique and unique scents where you experience the fragrances from glass testers, not on your skin. Nine perfumers have created 16 perfumes with names such as *Angéliques sous la pluie*, and *Musc Ravageur*. *Le Parfum de Thérèse*, described as 'complex and modern' was, in fact, created by the famous perfume creator, Edmond Roudnitska, some 40 years ago, but was never marketed because he made it exclusively for his wife. **Map p. 109, B7**

**Naila de Monbrison**, *6 Rue de Bourgogne, Tel: 01 47 05 11 15, Metro: Invalides*. If you are looking for something a bit different from classic up-market adornment, head for this address where contempo-rary and ethnically-inspired designs by young designers bring an original slant to quality jewellery. Monbrison brings together the creations of Dominique Modiano, Taher Chemirik, who is fast gathering a loyal following, the interior designer Mattia Bonetti, and Géraldine Luttenbacher whose sleek earrings, rings and necklaces are truly elegant. **Map p. 109, A6**

**Sabbia Rosa**, *71–73 Rue des Saints-Peres, Tel: 01 45 48 88 37, Metro: St-Germain des Prés*. Refined or sexy but always luscious, Sabbia Rosa lingerie comes in a vast range of colours, luxury fabrics, and minute attention to detail—a little lace here, some embroidery there, perhaps a bow or some feathers. Moana Moatti's made-to-measure undergarments and wonderful negligees and mules, are sought by some of the most glamorous stars and models—but, as you might expect, these beautiful things don't come cheap. **Map p. 109, B8**

# art glossary

### Art Brut

The term, invented by the artist Jean Dubuffet (1901–85), is described as 'outsider art' in English and applies to art produced by those who have no formal training and often on the margins of society. Examples of Art Brut work can be seen in the Pompidou Centre (*see p. 67*).

### Art Deco

A term coined in Paris after an exhibition of decorative and industrial art in 1925. Bold geometric shapes, rounded and streamlined are the hallmark of stylish Parisian buildings and furniture: the Hotel Lutetia was the first Art Deco hotel in Paris (*see p. 14*).

### Art Nouveau

Its sinuous vegetal forms and arabesques spread into architectural and interior design throughout Europe and North America at the end of the 19th century until World War I. Named after a Parisian shop of 1895 specialising in 'modern' goods, Art Nouveau synthesised earlier influences—Medieval, Celtic, the English Arts and Crafts Movement. The Musée Carnavalet has examples of this style (*see p. 72*). Art Nouveau was the style chosen by Hector Guimard for the first Métro station entrances of 1900.

### Arte Povera

An Italian expression first used in 1967 to cover a bewildering range of conceptual or minimalist art. Poor or worthless materials, such as torn newspapers and organic waste, are used to create another reality, thus liberating artists from conventional materials. Among exponents are Annis Kounellis, Giuseppe Penone and Mario Mertz (*see p. 67*).

### Baroque

During the 17th and 18th centuries, painting, sculpture and architecture came together in a spectacle of illusionism, dramatic lighting, shocking realism and grand perspectives. Baroque developed in southern Europe at the beginning of the 17th century, during the Counter-Reformation, to intensify the emotional propaganda of the Catholic Church. Rubens was the most important Baroque painter of the north (*see p.30*).

### Claude Lorrain (Claude Gellée; 1600–82)

The antidote to Nicolas Poussin (*see p. 134*), Claude's paintings are heavy in atmosphere and colour, composed to draw the eye in towards a distant horizon. Strong *chiaroscuro* and romantic landscapes or seascapes with elements of antique architecture are the setting for poetic visions of mythological events.

### Dada

One of the early revolts against traditional values in art and an expression of disillusionment following World War I, Dada involved anarchic group activity which mocked established criteria of style and materialism. It began in Switzerland c. 1915 and spread to New York, as well as the rest of Europe. A prominent figure in the Dada movement was Marcel Duchamp, whose *Fountain*, among other works, is shown in the Pompidou Centre (*see p. 66*).

### Delacroix, Eugène (1789–1863)

The major painter of the Romantic Movement in France who broke away from the classicising constraints of Jacques Louis David, admired Rubens and Veronese, and was a fan of English painters and writers such as Byron and Shakespeare. A visit to North Africa in 1832 opened his eyes to exotic colour and culture. Many later artists were influenced by Delacroix's handling of paint and use of colour. His frescoes can be seen in St-Sulpice (*see p. 97*).

### David, Jacques Louis (1748–1825)

The great Neoclassical painter and revered teacher, David was a deeply political figure, considered at the time to be both a revolutionary and an opportunist. His *Oath of the Horatii* made his reputation as an 'appeal to republican virtues and sentiments' although it was commissioned for the Crown, while *Brutus* was deliberately chosen to illustrate republicanism prior to the Revolution. Among his paintings

*a/s/e* Paris

depicting significant historical events, the *Tennis Court Oath* is an important example and can be seen in Musée Carnavalet (*see p. 71*).

### Expressionism

As a movement, this developed from the 1880s in Germany. In a wider context, it describes a heightened sense of emotion and passion on the part of the artist. Such intensity is most commonly expressed through the use of non-naturalistic colour. In this, Vincent van Gogh led the way, his Expressionist works can be seen in the Musée D'Orsay, and was expanded on by the Fauves (*see below*).

### Fauvism

Avant-garde movement characterised by the use of vibrant, non-naturalistic colours, which came to prominence in the years of great experimentation in art between the turn of the twentieth century and the First World War. A leading figure was Henri Matisse whose vibrant works can be seen in the Pompidou Centre (*see p. 64*).

### Futurism

This avant-garde artistic and literary movement, celebrated the contemporary world of speed and violence and attacking established values. It was founded by Tommaso Marinetti who published the Futurist Manifesto in 1909.

### Gothic

Gothic architecture was the predominant style throughout the Middle Ages until the early 15th century. It is characterised by the rib vault and flying buttress which enabled churches to be built to a great height by taking the strain off the walls. This also allowed huge stained glass windows to be inserted. Its beginnings are identified with the cathedral of St-Denis, c. 1140, and Notre-Dame (*see p. 86*). The description was first used pejoratively by the Italian painter Giorgio Vasari (1511–74). There was a Gothic revival in the 19th century.

### Impressionism

The word Impressionist was used derisively by a critic when Monet's *An Impression, Sunrise* was first exhibited in 1874. Impressionist painters sought to catch a mood and the play of light. They painted outdoors in front of the motif, and were interested in capturing a greater truth to nature and modern life as opposed to historical events. Colour research by the chemist Eugène Chevreul and the invention of ready-mixed paint in metal tubes and portable equipment were vital influences. The Impressionists lightened their palette, eliminating black and applied paint in juxtaposed dabs of colour. Impressionism opened the way to modernism and influenced many painters for a short time, whereas Monet, Pissarro and Sisley remained constant to the style. The Musée D'Orsay has an extensive collection of Impressionist works (*see p. 114*), as does the Musée de l'Orangerie (*see p. 47*).

### Manet, Edouard (1832–83)

After reacting violently against the Salon art (*see p. 135*) taught in the studio of the Academy painter Thomas Couture, Manet turned to subjects from contemporary life. Strongly influenced by Velázquez, Goya and Frans Hals, his work is characterised by strong contrasts, especially black and white, with few half-tones. There is a superb collection of his work at the Musée d'Orsay (*see p. 113*).

### Matisse, Henri (1869–1954)

Matisse's concern with colour began as a pupil of Gustav Moreau. It developed in association with painters such as Derain, Vlaminck and Signac, when he became leader of the Fauve movement (*see previous page*), characterised by an arbitrary, non-naturalistic use of vivid colour. Later he was deeply affected by Middle Eastern and North African art, and interiors, models and decorative flat patterns were the subjects of his work in Nice in the 1920s. His 'cut-outs' were a means of sculpting in colour, and he used this technique for his well-know *Jazz* series (*see p. 64*).

### Monet, Claude (1840–1926)

Leading Impressionist and the most dedicated to its aesthetics, Monet was a master of the visual sensation and how changes of light altered the mood of a motif, exemplified by his series paintings on show in the Musée de l'Orangerie (*see p. 47*). He was influenced by Japanese prints, studied with Pissarro and travelled to London, the Mediterranean and Venice. His reputation was established in the late 1880s. He created the gardens and lily ponds at his home in Giverny which provided endless inspiration from 1883.

### Neoclassicism

This term is applied to a theory of architecture which developed after the discovery of the ancient architectural treatise of Vitruvius in 1414. Architecture in the 17th century used a classical language which derived from ancient Greece and Rome. It is identified by the harmonious relationship of the parts to the whole and the use of elements such as columns and pediments. A fine example of Neoclassical architecture in Paris is the Panthéon (*see p. 95*).

### Picasso, Pablo (1881–1973)

The brilliant Spaniard, who settled in Paris in 1904, became one of the most dominant personalities of the 20th century in the visual arts. He was a brilliant reinterpreter of current artistic trends and a self-publicist. His contact with African art was a turning point in his work and led to a new pictorial form known as Cubism. He practised a Neoclassical style between the wars and was a brilliant draughtsman. His personal life was as varied as his professional one. He married the dancer Olga Khoklova in 1918, and Jacqueline Roque in 1961, and other long-term lovers deeply influenced his work. The Musée Picasso in Paris is dedicated to his life and career (*see p. 73*).

### Poussin, Nicolas (c. 1594–1665)

The greatest French classical painter was born in Normandy, but spent most of his life in Rome. He was successful in producing small works for the bourgeois élite, predominantly of mythological subjects. His carefully balanced figures probably owe their rather rigid poses to his use of a three-dimensional visual aid in the shape of a small stage with wax models. His works are well-represented in the Louvre (*see p. 30*).

### Renaissance

Meaning 'rebirth' or 'renewal', Renaissance ideas sprang from a reinterpretation of the values and culture of ancient Rome in Italy c.

1420. This meant a greater emphasis was placed on the individual than the preceding period, as well as on nature and philosophy. Renaissance architecture related more closely to the human scale, and painting synthesised Christianity, mythology and the mundane. The High Renaissance in art was a moment of intense harmony, emotion and truth to nature; works of this era are displayed in the Louvre.

## Rococo

This applies mainly to a light, curvy and playful decoration used in France during the 18th century, distinct from its predecessor, the heavyweight Baroque. The name originates from *rocaille* or shell-like forms. The style spread throughout interior décor and occasionally to the exterior of buildings in the 18th century. The Musée des Arts Décoratifs has examples of Rococo work (see p. 40).

## Rodin, Auguste (1840–1917)

One of the most celebrated sculptors of the late 19th century, Rodin started as a stone mason and in 1877 began to be noticed. A visit to Italy in 1875 and the influence of Michelangelo is seen in his *Gates of Hell*, (now in the Musée Rodin; see p. 121) commissioned in 1880 and completed only in 1917. Rodin had a profound influence on 20th-century sculpture although several artists (Maillot, Brancusi) made a deliberate effort to escape his spell.

## Salon

Artists of the Academy held their exhibitions in the Salon d'Apollon in the Louvre from the 17th century onwards but by the 19th century it was considered a stuffy and reactionary establishment which rejected the Impressionists and other avant-garde painters. They put up a fight and created alternative salons including the Salon des Refusés in 1863, which was followed by the Salons d'Automne and des Indépendants.

## School of Paris

A group of stylistically individual international artists in Paris between the wars. Picasso was among them, as were Modigliani, Soutine and Foujita, and later Antoni Tápies. Marc Chagall developed

Paris

a/s/e

a very personal, poetic imagery blending memories of his native Russia in *To Russia, Donkeys and Others* (1911). School of Paris works are collected in the Pompidou Centre.

## Surrealism

This movement of the 1920–30s penetrated the collective unconscious and rocked the visual arts. It developed from Dada, and was led by the writer André Breton who drew up the First Surrealist Manifesto in 1924. Breton defined the movement as 'pure psychic automatism'. It set out to break down the contradictions between the conscious and unconscious and drew inspiration from the writings of Sigmund Freud, dreams, found objects and their illogical juxtaposition. The Spanish artist Joan Miró was profoundly influenced by Surrealism, and some of his works can be seen in the Pompidou Centre (*see p. 66*).

## Symbolism

More a literary than a visual movement of the late 19th century, it gradually spread into the visual arts. Painters most closely associated with Symbolism were Puvis de Chavannes, Gustav Moreau, Odilon Redon, as well as Gauguin and the Pont-Aven Group in Brittany. A selection of Symbolist works can be seen in the Musée du Petit Palais (*see p. 44*).

## Toulouse-Lautrec, Henri de (1864–1901)

An aristocrat from southwest France, in Montmartre Lautrec absorbed the trends of the avant-garde art world. His studies of Parisian night life—dance halls and prostitutes in *maisons closes*—were compassionate, satirical or objective but titillated the public. He is best known for 32 revolutionary large poster designs using lithography (introduced in 1798).

# index

Numbers in italics are picture references. Numbers in bold denote major references.

The author would like to thank: Lesley Pullen and John Welz for their advice and input; also her Paris-based friends who have been so supportive: Marie Eymard, Yvonne Laugier-Werth and Renard and Hortense Meltz. Thanks are also due to Danièle Guyot of the Musées de la Ville de Paris, Pascale de Sèze of the Musée des Arts Décoratifs, Niko Melissano at the Louvre, Jean-Claude Lalumière at the Musée d'Orsay, Anne Le Floch at the Petit Palais, and Clémence Goldberger at the Musée Rodin, as well as the French Tourist Offices in London and Paris.

## And if you have enjoyed your visit to Paris and want to find out more, try our

# BLUE GUIDE PARIS

Blue Guides® have been a leading publisher of cultural guide books for 90 years. Our 480-page all-colour Blue Guide Paris, also by Delia Gray-Durant, is the definitive reference book for the returning traveller who wants to know, understand and enjoy more of Paris.

Available from our website: www.blueguides.com and from all good bookshops, £15.95 / US$29.95.

The author and the publisher have made reasonable efforts to ensure
the accuracy of all the information in art/shop/eat Paris; however, they can
accept no responsibility for any loss, injury or inconvenience sustained by
any traveller as a result of information or advice contained in the guide.

Every effort has been made to contact the copyright owners of material
reproduced in this guide. We would be pleased to hear from any copyright
owners we have been unable to reach.

Statement of editorial independence: Blue Guides Limited, their authors
and editors, are prohibited from accepting any payment from any hotel,
restaurant, gallery or other establishment for its inclusion in this guide, or
for a more favourable mention than would otherwise have been made.

art/shop/eat Paris
Fully rewritten second edition 2008

Published by Blue Guides Limited, a Somerset Books Company
49–51 Causton St, London SW1P 4AT
www.artshopeat.com
www.blueguides.com
© Blue Guides Limited
Blue Guides is a registered trademark

ISBN 978-1-905131-21-1

Editor: Sophie Livall

Photo editor: Róbert Szabó Benke
Layout and design: Anikó Kuzmich, Regina Rácz, Katalin Seregélyes
Maps: Dimap Bt
Floor plans: Imre Bába
Printed in Singapore by Tien Wah Press Pte

Photo credits: p. 143, which forms part of this copyright page

We welcome all comments, corrections and views. We want to hear all
feedback, and as a mark of gratitude we will be happy to send a free copy of
one of our books to anyone providing useable corrections, constructive
criticism, or gross flattery. Please contact us via the website,
www.artshopeat.com

SOMERSET BOOKS